A Travel Odyssey

ACADEMY PACIFIC

Travel College

1777 NORTH VINE STREET, LOS ANGELES, CA 90028

A Travel Odyssey

The ACADEMY PACIFIC *Story*

William A. Schoneberger

THE
DONNING COMPANY
PUBLISHERS

❋ DEDICATION ❋

Dedicated to

Esther Sampson Myers

for her warmth and kindness during Marsha Sampson's teenage years when Esther
and her husband Charles graciously and warmly served as surrogate parents.

Copyright © 1997 by William A. Schoneberger ✈
Second printing (paperback) 1997
Third printing (paperback) 1999

For information, write:
THE DONNING COMPANY/PUBLISHERS
184 Business Park Drive, Suite 106
Virginia Beach, VA 23462

Steve Mull, *General Manager*
Barbara Bolton, *Project Director*
Tracey Emmons-Schneider, *Director of Research*
Kevin M. Brown, *Senior Graphic Designer*
Dawn V. Kofroth, *Assistant General Manager*
Tony Lillis, *Editor*
Teri S. Arnold, *Senior Marketing Coordinator*

Library of Congress Cataloging-in-Publication Data

Schoneberger, William A., 1926-
A Travel Odyssey : the Academy Pacific story / William A. Schoneberger.
p. cm.
Includes index.
ISBN 0-89865-989-2 (alk. paper)
ISBN 1-57864-023-7 (pbk: alk. paper)
1. Academy Pacific (Hollywood, Los Angeles, Calif.) 2. Tourist trade -- Study and teaching --
California. 3. Toy, Marsha Sampson.
I. Title.
G155.U6S36   1997
338.4'791071'5--dc21   97-3366
                                                           CIP

✖ CONTENTS ✖

The Career College

Over the past eleven years I have had the delightful opportunity to represent a little-known sector of education that has positively and dramatically impacted literally millions of adults and young adults each year—private career colleges and schools. This is a unique sector of education. Through the use of private capital and a strong market-responsive philosophy, these institutions provide to individuals the skills they need to upgrade their capabilities or begin new and fulfilling careers. By providing individuals the technical skills they need to enter their chosen employment fields in the shortest possible time, at the least possible cost, everyone benefits—the student, the employer and the taxpayer.

The reason that many of the owners of these private career colleges and schools are so successful and play such a major role in meeting the needs of employers is that they themselves were originally in that field of endeavor. They now pass their knowledge onto those eager to join their ranks. Many owners of career colleges and schools have been artisans, craftpersons and technicians. They are now teachers and mentors. All successful owners and directors understand the world of work and the critical role that ethics, accountability and serving their customer really means in achieving success in the marketplace.

Stephen J. Blair

Past President and CEO, Career College Association
Past President and CEO, National Association of Trade and Technical Schools
Director, Division of Policy and Program Development, U.S. Department of Education

N

O ONE INDIVIDUAL PERSONIFIES MORE OF THE VERY POSITIVE ASPECTS
of private career education than Marsha Sampson Toy.

What follows in this lovely publication are the delightful stories that have made
up the life of this remarkable person. What you will miss in the reading are the
sparkling eyes and the animation that so permeate Marsha's telling of her stories.
But that is all. Her adventures as one of the first flight attendants in the fledgling
commercial aviation industry, her nurses training that enabled her to fulfill her
dream of flying and how she learned to fly are all here. The need after the war for
trained flight attendants, the school that she set up to meet the demand, and the difficulties in making the business work are also here. What will become evident as
you read this story are Marsha Toy's relentless commitment to quality and the highest standards of personal and business ethics.

The chapters on the Academy Pacific and how it conducts the business of career
education will give the reader an opportunity to understand why millions of individuals have chosen and will continue to choose this form of education and learning to
advance their own career paths. Through this understanding, parents can see the
tremendous value of such a nurturing learning environment and its possibilities for
their own children, and for that matter, for themselves.

Most importantly, this story will give you a chance to meet a person with a rare
and delightful zest for life; a person who has had to overcome physical pain and
business failures, created a superb learning and nurturing environment, and continues the grand adventure of life with unmitigated joy. It is my pleasure to introduce
to you a person I deem it a great honor to call my friend, Marsha Sampson Toy. ✈

Stephen J. Blair

A S THE RESEARCH EVOLVED FOR THIS BOOK, IT BECAME INCREASINGLY evident to me that Marsha Toy's life and dedication to her school were something special. I was aware of her business acumen and dedication to social responsibility through my association with her on the Board of Directors of the Aero Club of Southern California and her work on the Board of Travelers Aid of Los Angeles.

What I couldn't know until work on this book began was Marsha Toy's commitment to *teaching* young people, guiding careers that might otherwise be dead ends.

Thanks to those on the Aero Club Board who knew of Marsha Toy's achievements—Harlan Jost, Arvin Basnight, Linda Dozier, Nissen Davis, Vi Rigby and Jim Ragsdale. To those whom I tapped for information about Marsha Toy and the school—Alma Lynton, Cynthia Ann Rodriguez, Judie Parr Graham-Bell, Sandra Moyer, Patricia Benchouchan—my heartiest appreciation for their candor.

Without the staff of Academy Pacific who "laid it all out" for me—Dan Gilreath, Sandi Dover, Paul Favreau, Kathy Miller—this book could not have been written. However, the greatest praise—and thanks—for his over and above effort go to Doug Barr, the liaison and "Mr. Inside" for Academy Pacific. He was collaborator *par excellence.*

My most valued professional counsel came from my college co-editor, personal friend of nearly 50 years, and an author in his own right, Doug Smith of Greenville, South Carolina.

Finally, initial encouragement for this book and the odyssey of Marsha Toy—as well as valuable editing together with advice, counsel and critiquing during the writing—came from my wife, Patricia L. Schoneberger. ✈

William A. Schoneberger
Malibu, California
December, 1996

THE COURSE OF ONE'S LIFETIME IS HARDLY EVER A STRAIGHT AND NARROW path leading toward a single, preordained destination. Looking back over eight decades—or even as few as two decades—most people reflect on their life as a series of detours, of side roads, of meandering off the beaten path and, frequently, of including a sharp change of direction.

Raised as one of twelve children during the often difficult but certainly impression-marking days of the Depression years in America in the 1930s, the high ethical and moral standards of that era were indelibly stamped on Marsha Sampson Toy. She is a living example of a philosophy espoused by a learned professor of humanities: *What you are is where you were when!* For this concept, people raised during the Depression era are the easiest to identify and those years the most definitive. (Subsequent examples of "What you ares" are, of course, Baby Boomers and Generation X.)

For all the obvious and recognized reasons, Marsha "Sammy" Sampson Toy's interaction with her family, her nurse's training, her air hostess experiences as well as her managerial duties and exposure at a newly-opened air base all combined to prepare her for her eventual career as a *teacher*.

Like most other people, she had no idea that these life experiences would shape her ultimate career choice. As another homespun philosopher put it, "She wears the class colors of the school of experience, black and blue!"

Ironically, when contemplating what she wanted to do in the mid-thirties, Sammy was aware that the paths open to women at that time were essentially limited to secretarial, nursing or teaching. As she later admitted, she "certainly didn't want to be a *teacher*," so she selected nurses' training.

However, happily for the more than 25,000 graduates of Academy Pacific, the confluence of Marsha Toy's varied background and the high standards of her family came together in 1948 in Hollywood, California, with the founding of the Marsha Toy Air Hostess School, later to become Academy Pacific Travel College. All of those influences and experiences of the previous thirty years came together in the establishment of the school. The tenets established in the early years have been expanded, embellished and honed to perfection in today's Academy Pacific. ✈

The Sampson clan, Christmas 1912; Albert Sampson (with mustache), 3rd row, left; Annie Sampson, holding baby Melvin, over his left shoulder; Grandfather Sampson (with beard), center

ONE

THE PENNSYLVANIA STREET KID

"In my very own self, I am part of my family."
David H. Lawrence

REMEMBER LILLIAN GILBREATH'S BOOK, *CHEAPER BY THE DOZEN?*

Long before it became a bestseller in the 1950s, the Sampson family of Wilkinsburg, Pennsylvania, was a living example of that legendary Gilbreath family.

Marsha "Sammy" Sampson (Toy) was the ninth of 12 children born to Albert L. and Annie Hormel Sampson. (Originally Christened Martha, she later officially changed her name to Marsha.) That fateful event was August 9, 1915. Marsha Toy says today, "I'm sure glad my Mother and Father decided when they were married they were going to have twelve children, because I was number nine in line and, if they'd not decided to have a dozen, I probably wouldn't be here."

The senior Sampsons even decided on six boys and six girls—and that's how it turned out. The oldest, Belle, whom Marsha says still tries to run things in the Sampson family, was 96 in 1996. Belle led the five surviving Sampson sisters on a 1993 junket to Hawaii, with the five "girls" tooling through Los Angeles International and Honolulu airports in their wheel chairs, drawing whistles and cheers as they were driven in the "chairs" to board a jetliner. (*Ed. note: Belle, age 96, died in October, 1996.*) Aside from Belle and Marsha, other Sampson "girls" are Esther, Beulah, Ruth and the baby who died as an infant. The sons were Kenneth, Glenn, Orin, Stanley and Harold plus Melvin who died at age 10 as a result of an accidental gunshot.

Founder, president and First Lady of Academy Pacific Travel College, Marsha "Sammy" Sampson Toy's Mother and Father were parents who, in today's terminology would be called "role models." They set standards not only for Marsha but for her brothers and sisters as well.

Marsha says, "I probably had the most fabulous Father and Mother ever born." Her Scottish-Irish Father was "wonderful, loving who just knew how to handle all of us. But, wow, did we do whatever he wanted us to do because we knew he meant what he said."

"He had various businesses," she said about her Father. "He had a home construction business, ran crews who built homes, had farm land which he rented for cattle raising, started a savings and loan and even operated a coal mine."

Annie, Albert Sampson, Marsha Sampson Toy's parents, c. 1898.

RIGHT PAGE: *Annie Hormel Sampson, Marsha Toy's mother, c. 1890.*

Marsha's brothers learned independence — and the construction business — from their father. One of the Sampson brothers, Orin, who had demonstrated his business acumen early (as a young boy delivering the *Pittsburgh Press*, later establishing a newspaper distributorship, including supervising other teens, raising chickens, selling eggs, making and selling ice cream, even opening a local grocery store) started what was to become a family construction business. Ultimately including four Sampson brothers, the post-World War II business became Pennsylvania's largest home building company. Reflecting principles derived from their family's heritage, they built entire communities, including the local church, community swimming pool and recreation facilities.

From their father the brothers had learned "If you want to earn in this life, you've got to work. Nobody gives you allowances." According to Marsha, her Father said to her brothers (and to her): "I'll tell you what you might think about. You can try it if you want." He offered an option.

Attributing her lifetime of high ethical standards to her Father's influence, Marsha Toy recalls that when she was laying the foundation for today's Academy Pacific, she was often faced with decisions about which path to take: the easier (but sometimes ethically questionable) or the straightforward, honest road. "Each time I would think, 'what would my Father have done?'" The question was always answered: "I went over to the straightforward, honest side. So, he continues to be my inspiration.

"It's too bad everyone can't have great parents like mine."

Sammy's mother, Annie Hormel Sampson was of German stock who lived by the phrase *Erst die arbeit dann das spiel* (First the work, then the play). Marsha describes her as "one of those really hard-working German women ... who tended her own garden, did the washing and ironing and made our clothes ... in addition to loving, caring for and rearing a dozen children."

The strict, church-going Presbyterian parents set standards for their family that would endure for all of their lives — standards that affect today's Academy Pacific through Marsha Toy's original, and continuing, tenets. Her entrepreneurial spirit, sense of adventure, dedication and, of course, the work ethic learned from her Pennsylvania Presbyterian parents, are reflected in the way she continues her direction of the School. Marsha Toy's caring about those around her as well as her ability to relate to others was shaped in those formative years of the 1920s and 1930s when she grew up as one of a dozen Sampson children.

Sampson family, nine children, Marsha Toy center front, 1918.

But, life for the Sampson family wasn't all work and no play. They had fun, too. The senior Sampson, who dabbled in a wide range of businesses was, among other things, a competent builder who designed and constructed the family homestead in Wilkinsburg (now Penn Hills, a Pittsburgh suburb). Father Sampson kept adding rooms as his family kept expanding. The homestead, still standing, ended up as one of the larger manses in Wilkinsburg, with 15 rooms — a veritable Sampson Manor House.

Even in the face of tragedy, the Sampsons managed to have fun. When one of her twelve children, a 10-year old boy, was accidentally shot by another youngster, Annie Sampson was devastated. So in 1923, Father Sampson decided a change of scenery was in order. He packed up the ten children (a baby girl had died in

Five Sampson sons, five daughters; Marsha Toy center, 1939 (two children had died).

infancy), chartered a railroad passenger car and took the family on a rail trip from Pittsburgh to Los Angeles. The four day and night trip in a rail car that included seven state rooms and an equal number of berths was marked by hilarity, spit ball-throwing and a plethora of generally active children roaming the train as well as the stops along the way.

But Mother and Father Sampson, mindful of fellow train travelers, kept a close rein on their offspring.

The family had relatives in Eagle Rock, a Los Angeles suburb. They rented a house there. Always the entrepreneur, Albert Sampson began to acquire property and build homes in the area.

But the Sampsons began to get restless. Some wanted to return to Pittsburgh; others wanted to stay in the land of milk and honey. Considering his very democratic family, Father Sampson decided to take a vote.

Eldest sister Belle (remember her; the one who even at 96 is still an operations director) had a boyfriend in Pittsburgh and her heart told her to return there. So,

Sampsons stayed in Eagle Rock home, 1923.

Sampson Pennsylvania mountain vacation home, 1936.

assuming the role of a young lobbyist, she quietly (and separately) figuratively twisted the arms of her siblings to vote to return. As Marsha puts it, "She almost forced us to vote 'yes' to go back. We were a little afraid of her." The vote went her way.

Albert Sampson bought a Model A Ford and, with two of his teenage sons and a teenage daughter began the eastward cross-country trip. They camped along the way, shot jack rabbits for food and had a wonderful time because their Father was fun, an inspiration and a ringleader.

Back in Wilkinsburg, the elder Sampson quickly re-established his leadership in the community, raising money for the Presbyterian Church, setting up a choir, including the choirmaster and his wife, and helping to build a church that even today

Sammy (Marsha Sampson Toy), 1934.

Sammy, sister Ruth, Pennsylvania corn field, 1931.

stands in Penn Hills. The churchyard has the graves of several of the Sampson family, including Marsha's Mother and Father.

Father Albert Sampson died at age 64 in 1930; his wife, Annie, followed only two years later. By then some of the Sampsons were off and married, so Marsha at age 15 was chief cook and bottle washer for those in the clan still at home trying to hold things together.

When a couple of the older boys married, they and two married sisters "drew straws to see who got me, my sister and the two younger brothers," according to Marsha. During her days as a "surrogate daughter" to one of her sisters, Esther Myers, Marsha graduated from Wilkinsburg High School in 1933.

As she tells it, "In those days there wasn't much choice for women; essentially three: teacher, secretary or nurse. Secretary seemed dull to me. And I said the *last thing* I ever wanted to do was be a teacher, be associated with any school, so that left nursing."

Marsha entered nurses' training in 1933, graduating in 1936. Her strict, high moral-standards, tough training took place at Presbyterian Hospital on Pittsburgh's north side. Dressed in what she describes as "flower sack dresses, black cotton

Nursing class, Presbyterian Hospital, Pittsburgh, 1933; Sammy standing, far right.

Nursing school roommates, 1935; Sammy second from left.

Nursing students home on leave, Pittsburgh, 1936; Sammy far right.

Nursing graduate Sammy Sampson (Marsha Toy), 1937.

Registered Nurse diploma, 1937.

Sampson brothers builders, Harold, non-relative, Glenn, Stanley, c. 1950.

stockings and 'old lady' black shoes, with a white bib that went in front," Marsha and her fellow nurse trainees cleaned bed pans, changed and scrubbed beds and floors and were generally treated as indentured servants. They went on field trips to slaughter houses (to make sure they could stand the sight of blood and guts), witnessed surgery in the operating room, and visited mental institutions to observe patients. Marsha recalls one mental home patient who surreptitiously, but happily, confided in the assembled nursing students she had just come down from Mars.

Under the stern, demanding eyes of nursing supervisors, trainees were routinely given the toughest jobs. Marsha recalls one patient, a syphilitic former madam, who was suffering dementia and in the final stages of her life. "She was just the meanest woman I ever met. I was timid and, of course, intimidated by her former profession and all it implied. With my supervisor looking on, I made her bed with a required folded, carefully measured corner. When I finished I knew it was done to perfection. The madam promptly kicked all the covers and sheets on the floor. She knew what she was doing; she was tormenting me."

Early settlers Harold, Mrs. Kenneth, Kenneth Sampson, reunion, 1978.

Brother Builders, Pittsburgh Press, 1953.

Marsha Toy at wheel of Ford Touring Car, 1991.

Sampson family reunion, 1985, Marsha Toy, front, second right.

The Sampson clan, Pittsburgh, 1991; Marsha Toy seated center, white blouse.

The same madam, whose vanity wig Marsha carefully fitted on her head, making sure it made her appear as appealing as possible, waited patiently until Marsha was done fitting it on her head. Then she promptly spun around the wig, wearing it backward for the benefit of her two-nurse audience.

Over the three-year schooling, trainees were allowed out one night a week (with a midnight curfew), one overnight a month if they had a letter from a parent or guardian; were housed six to a room and had a 10 p.m. bedcheck every night, carried out by a stern-faced supervisor waving a flashlight. "We didn't want to waste time eating so we lowered bed sheets out the window so boys below could tie in a sack of hamburgers, then we'd hoist it in, enjoying a 'forbidden feast' in our rooms," she recalls.

Although regular staff normally prepared bodies for the morgue if a patient expired on their floor, one nighttime shift only trainee Marsha and a fellow student were on duty when a man died. They knew the requirements for corpse preparation, but in this strict Presbyterian environment they had never even bathed the "private parts" of a male patient (leaving that task to the patient himself), let alone 'prepped' one for the morgue. They tried in vain to reach male orderlies elsewhere in the hospital. But, it was the middle of the night; the place was short staffed. No one could come to their rescue.

Marsha and her compatriot, Rosabelle Painter, did all the routine prepping, right up to the 'critical area.' Faced with that challenge, with conspiratorial fervor, they decided to tie it off, using three-inch gauze that was standard for all other preparations. As the task progressed, they began to giggle, finally fashioning a huge, decorative bow, using gauze as ribbon.

"We covered him with a mortuary shroud, did the necessary paperwork, loaded him on a gurney, wheeled the body down to the morgue, then slid him into one of the metal drawers where the body would await an autopsy. You know, Rosabelle, the funeral parlor guys will probably get a kick out of this," she confidently assured her co-conspirator.

They went back to the third floor.

Little more than two hours later, the phone rang at the nurses' station. A booming voice, announcing himself as the morgue's pathologist, wanted to know who took care of the male patient from that floor who had expired.

"In a timid voice, I said 'me.'"

"Who is 'me?'" asked the doctor.

"Miss Sampson," Marsha replied, a touch of fear in her voice. By then she was scared to death, knowing she and her compatriot, Rosabelle, would probably be dismissed as a result of their practical joke.

"Who else was with you?"

"Miss Painter," Marsha squeaked out.

"Thank you," he replied and hung up.

"I told Rosabelle to get her bags packed since we were about to be kicked out of the hospital because of all those holier-than-thou nurses and administrators who wouldn't see anything funny about our decorations."

But to the amazement of both nurse trainees, they never *heard* another word about the incident. They did, however, notice that all the doctors and interns with business on the third floor, after they identified Miss Sampson and Miss Painter, could hardly contain their laughter.

With her graduate nurse's hat firmly and proudly implanted on her head, Marsha went on private duty–in homes and hospitals. Routine at other hospitals was not much different from Presbyterian, but house calls gave Marsha another view of life that contrasted sharply with the environment in which she had been raised. The house call duty may have been her first exposure to the fact that not all families, parents and children were like hers. The perspectives derived from home health care during those days provided her an even more humanitarian recognition of families different from her own.

But nursing also provided a direct path to an aviation career that would take Sammy (Marsha Sampson Toy) to the far reaches of the world. Moreover, despite her protestations that "The last thing I ever wanted to be was a teacher," the roots of educating others had already begun to grow. ✈

TWO

THE GLAMOUR OF AVIATION

"Travel is fatal to prejudice, bigotry and narrow-mindedness."
Mark Twain

"I HEARD OVER THE RADIO THAT THEY WERE PUTTING REGISTERED NURS-
es on board airplanes because they wanted the public not to be afraid to fly. They
felt if there was a registered nurse on board that would help psychologically,"
recalls Marsha Sampson Toy about her first inkling of the romance and glamour of
flying.

It was 1937. Sammy had been practicing her registered nursing skills for nearly
two years when she heard that radio report.

"Wow! That's for me. Wouldn't that be wonderful flying on an airplane. Here's
an opportunity to travel and get paid for it. This would be just wonderful ... glamorous ... exciting. So I started trying to get one of those jobs. In those days there
were United, American and TWA. That was it."

Those radio announcements, combined with Sammy Sampson's nurses' education and training, became the early nourishment for the roots that were subcon-
sciously being planted for Academy Pacific.

Anytime she heard one of those three embryonic airlines was interviewing and
hiring she climbed in her 1934 Ford, driving to New York or Chicago. Her search
for airline employment lasted for nearly two years. Although she kept being reject-
ed by the stoic males who conducted the interviews, Sammy persevered, going back
time and again. She recited all her years of nurses' training as well as her "mother-
ing" of her large family in an effort to convince those hard-nosed interviewers that
she should be chosen as one of their new crop of air hostesses. Nothing seemed to
impress them, however.

"I never quit going back. I honestly think TWA hired me because they were just
sick of seeing me back again. If I were one of those interviewers, I think I would
have said: 'you might as well hire her.'"

United Airlines (then a unit of giant Boeing Air and Transport Company) pioneered the first inflight attendant when the now-famous Ellen Church began flying
for United in May 1930. American and TWA, quickly recognizing the merits of the

LEFT PAGE: ***Air Hostess Sammy Sampson (Marsha Toy), TWA DC-2, 1939.***

comfort psychology of having a nurse aboard as well as the addition of personalized service for their seven to fourteen passengers, followed the lead of their competitor.

Finally, after two years of perseverance, Sammy received a telegram, followed by a confirming letter from Transcontinental and Western Airways, *the Lindbergh*

Sammy Sampson, first car; drove to airline interviews, 1937.

Line, that she had been selected for air hostess training. She was asked to report to Kansas City (then headquarters for the airline) for her final, acceptance interview. The airline would even pick up the fare as well as her hotel room. Since they served Pittsburgh, she could "hop, skip and jump" in a DC-3 to Kansas City direct from her hometown.

But Sammy knew there was a problem. From weight standards she already had memorized, she believed she was *at least* 15 pounds overweight. "They would put me on a scale and that would be it."

Ingeniously, she wired TWA, acknowledging her selection, but stating she had a patient who insisted she remain with her for another two weeks until the patient was over her crisis. Could TWA please extend her appointment for two weeks?

"I went on a crash diet. I didn't eat for two weeks. The weight just fell off. By then, I was ready for 'em."

In October 1938, Sammy Sampson, age 23, reported to TWA in Kansas City for her final interview and to begin air hostess training. But the hiring process had one more surprise.

Following her hiring interview, Sammy and her fellow air hostess hirees were herded into a room, then asked to strip naked for an examination by a woman doctor. "I don't know if they could get by with that today, but we all accepted it. We walked back and forth, turned around and were generally visually examined by the female doctor so she could see our actual measurements, our posture, etc.

"I really wanted that job. I was going to do what they asked, but it sure went against everything I was ever brought up with. Even with such a big family, we were *never* allowed to show our bodies–even to our sisters. We learned to take off our clothes under our nightgown. Even my nurses' training hadn't prepared me for that. I'll never forget it."

When Sammy went into TWA training the airline had about eighty air hostesses flying their various routes around the United States. During that period they were operating DC-2s and DC-3s. Training for air hostesses took six weeks. Training and classes were held in a large Kansas City TWA hangar in offices and a classroom high above the hangar floor.

When she completed the air hostess course, Sammy was sent to San Francisco. She didn't select the destination. TWA had an accident near Las Vegas in which an entire crew was killed. Nobody wanted to be assigned to replace this San Francisco-based crew. So a mandate came down from above that the new hires would go as replacements.

Transcontinental & Western Air, Inc. hiring letter, 1938.

That San Francisco assignment was fortuitous. It was her first working venture to the West Coast. She would eventually meet her husband. It planted her California roots. And, the assignment raised her exposure to TWA and its management.

The airline was just establishing an air mail/passenger route between San Francisco and Phoenix with stops in Boulder City (where Boulder Dam had just been completed) and Las Vegas (before the opening of some of the early and famous casinos). Because of the terminus in Phoenix, Sammy and her air hostess cohorts had to find living quarters there.

By the luck of the draw the newly-commissioned air hostess was on the inaugural San Francisco-Phoenix flight. "I was scared to death," she said. "In Phoenix they had even arranged mounted cowboys for me to hand the mail out of the airplane. complete with picture taking."

With the usual pomp and ceremony, the inaugural flight included key TWA management. Jack Frye, then president, and T.B. Wilson, board chairman. Frye, aside from his leadership role as TWA president, is also an aviation history icon as the author of the now-famous two paragraph letter to Donald W. Douglas asking for a quote on development and purchase of a two-engine transport capable of carrying fourteen passengers. It was that letter that sparked the beginning of the Douglas DC-1, -2, -3 series of transports. This single page, two paragraph letter was the only request for quotation (RFQ) required to set in motion one of the most successful aircraft programs in history.

INTEROFFICE CORRESPONDENCE
TRANSCONTINENTAL & WESTERN AIR, INC.

TO: Miss Martha V. Sampson   LOCATION: Kansas City

LOCATION: San Francisco   DATE: November 3, 1938

SUBJECT:

PLEASE QUOTE FILE NO.

This will confirm your employment as an Air Hostess, effective October 18, 1938, at a salary of $100.00 per month. You are being employed subject to a probationary period of 90 days, which should be ample to prove your ability to handle the hostess work to which you are assigned. The Company reserves the right to terminate your employment without advance notice and without liability for wages or salary except such as may have been earned prior to such termination at any time during the probationary period or at the expiration of the probationary period.

The Passenger Service Manual should be used as a ready reference manual, and you should learn and understand the contents of this Manual. One of the most important regulations covering your employment is that you are not to accept "tips" and we trust you will abide by this rule.

With the preliminary training you have received, and your attention to details, plus your desire to make every passenger a TWA booster, I feel sure you will make a success of your work.

If you have difficulties of any kind, doubts regarding procedure, trouble with your paper work, tickets or manifests, one of the Chief Hostesses or myself will be glad to assist you at any time.

C. A. Williams
Supt. of Passenger Service

CAW:HM
cc: L. G. Fritz
    L. M. Reed
    Adele D. Jenkins

TWA employment confirmation; $100 per month, 1938.

INTEROFFICE CORRESPONDENCE
TRANSCONTINENTAL & WESTERN AIR, INC.

TO: Martha V. Sampson   LOCATION: Kansas City

LOCATION: Kansas City   DATE: March 11, 1939

SUBJECT:

PLEASE QUOTE FILE NO.

We are sending hostess-representatives to the San Francisco Exposition for its duration. On March 15th, Miss Ice will be there for one month, and then will be replaced by another hostess. This turnover will continue until the Fair ends. After carefully looking over our list of hostesses, we have selected you as one whom we wish to have represent TWA at this Fair. Selections were based on these qualifications:

1. Good personal appearance in uniform.
2. Ability to sell TWA service.
3. Past cooperation in traffic assignments.

The salary will be the same, and in addition, you will be allowed one dollar ($1.00) per day relief expense, but no moving expense.

The hours have not been decided upon, but Mr. Ernie Smith is arranging the time as he believes will be most agreeable with at least one day off duty each week. He will help you find suitable living quarters in downtown San Francisco and furnish transportation from the Ferry House to the Fair and return. You will be given at least two weeks' notification. An immediate reply will be appreciated.

We hope that you will accept this assignment and will find it refreshing and entertaining.

Gladys Entrekin
Chief Air Hostess

GE:HM

TWA sends Sammy to San Francisco Exposition, $1 per day expenses, one day off per week, 1939.

INTEROFFICE CORRESPONDENCE
TRANSCONTINENTAL & WESTERN AIR, INC.

To: .Martha V. Sampson   SF   LOCATION: .Kansas City

OUR FILE NO.   DATE: May 24, 1939

SUBJECT   IN REPLY PLEASE QUOTE FILE NO.

You completed your first six months' employment by TWA on April 18, 1939, and the effective date of your salary increase from $115.00 to $125.00 per month is May 1, 1939.

Within the six-month period, you have steadily progressed in efficient handling of hostess duties, and have earned several letters of commendation.

I am very happy to have you join the first year class and will look forward to giving you your one-year hostess service pin in another six months.

Gladys Entrekin
Chief Air Hostess

GE:HM
cc: L. G. Fritz
    L. M. Reed
    C. A. Williams

Six months raise, from $115 to $125 per month, 1939.

Following that inaugural flight, Frye and Wilson and their families became regular passengers on those San Francisco-Phoenix runs. "We only had one flight a day going each way and there were only four flight attendants there. I could hardly miss. So, I got to know the top brass pretty well. It was a case of being in the right place at the right time," Sammy recalls.

Another fond memory from those days in the late 1930s brings a smile to Marsha's face. It was the first opportunity in her life to save any money.

"Our hotels and meals were taken care of and we all had boyfriends who took us to dinner. Our rent was split four ways, so I began accumulating money." Her pay was eighty dollars per month. Moreover, since that was before hourly restrictions were imposed, work time was the hours required to fly the route plus pre- and post-flight time.

Her newfound accumulated wealth burned a hole in her pocket, so to speak. Targeting five hundred dollars as her goal, Sammy decided that when she reached that magic mark, she would go to Hawaii. The songs and romance of the islands beckoned. But, although Pan American Airways flew the Pacific to Hawaii in their famous China Clippers, there were no *interchange passes* in those days; TWA flight privileges couldn't be exchanged. So a sea cruise on the *Coolidge* became her transportation of choice.

With her innate enthusiasm she confided in TWA Board Chairman Wilson, who was on one of her San Fran-Phoenix flights, about her trip to the islands and how she was going.

Sammy Sampson's potential as a public relations plus for TWA was apparently recognized in the hallowed halls of Kansas City. Her air hostess duties on the inaugural San Fran-Phoenix flight that included as passengers both the chairman and president of the airline had not gone unnoticed. When she enthusiastically informed Chairman Wilson of her Hawaii intentions, he promptly relayed the intelligence back to Kansas City along with a strong suggestion that Sammy be utilized by TWA.

TWA Air Hostesses on indoctrination tour, Hollywood, 1938.

This word that came down from on high was enough for the airline's public relations department to take action. In Kansas City there was considerable nodding in the affirmative that this idea certainly made sense to *them.*

Theon Wright, TWA's public relations director, called Sammy. He casually informed her they wanted to do a story on her trip to Honolulu. However, he was forthright enough to tell her the airline wanted to begin serving Honolulu and "we want to get some publicity out there."

Mr. Wright (no relation to brothers of the same name who in 1903 achieved powered flight on the sand dunes of Kitty Hawk, North Carolina) had another sur-

prise for Sammy. A vote had been taken in Kansas City and she had been elected *Miss Aviation*!

With that news, hundreds of questions came immediately to Sammy's mind. They were soon answered. Her newly-crowned title brought her duties as a glamorous spokesperson for the airline, complete with pictures of her at her duties on TWA's DC-2s as well as ultimately picturing her embarkation and Pacific voyage aboard the *Coolidge*.

Despite pre-Pearl Harbor security precautions, the influential TWA Hawaii public relations contractor, Earl Thacker, was able to board the ship even before it docked. Thacker told Sammy of her many and varied duties on the island as *Miss Aviation*.

Upon docking in Honolulu a chauffeured car whisked her off to the Royal Hawaiian Hotel, right on the beach at Waikiki. Her suite was filled with flowers. Her phone rang persistently; she was being asked for interviews and quotes by eager reporters who had been alerted by Thacker. Pretty heady stuff for a young, naive girl from Wilkinsburg, Pennsylvania.

The power of company public relations in those pre-World War II days was impressive. There were lots of pictures and stories in the Honolulu newspapers about the arrival of *Miss Aviation*. Even Dole Pineapple–the pillar of the islands' economy–got in on the act. A photo of Sammy drinking Dole Pineapple juice while reposing on the lanai of the Royal Hawaiian moved via wire service to the mainland. It appeared in the *Pittsburgh Press*. Senior sister Belle, of course, saw it and promptly warned her younger sister about the perils of drinking whiskey.

The caption on that photo included the revealing fact that *Miss Aviation*, who had gone by sea from San Francisco to Hawaii, had never in her life been on any water bigger than a pond behind her home. Sammy Sampson had her first lesson in the art of spin doctors who could readily conjure up tales that helped peddle stories.

Sammy's next lesson in press relations came on the beach at Waikiki. She'd spread her beach towel, preparing to catch a few rays of the wonderful Hawaiian sun. She was soon joined by another young woman who told Sammy she looked familiar; what did she do? Sammy proudly told her she was an air hostess for TWA. With the glamour of aviation still in its embryonic stages, the woman evidenced natural curiosity about Sammy's flying experiences.

"Have you had any hair-raising experiences?" the young sun bather asked innocently.

Sammy confided in her fellow beach companion that one time she'd been alone at the rear of a DC-2 when the back door flew open, leaving an opening of more than a foot. Although the door hadn't torn itself off, the speed and outside pressure

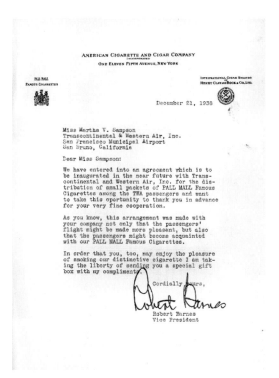

Air Hostesses were "tobacco pushers" in 1938.

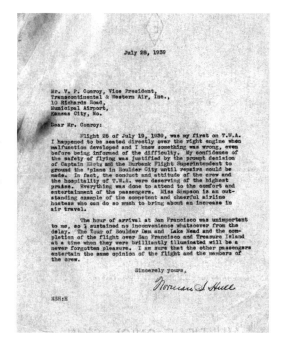

Commendation letter for Miss Sampson, 1939.

Left Page: *Miss Aviation cared for twin New York-California passengers, 1940.*

Martha Zanover, Sammy Sampson, TWA Air Hostesses (with S. Carruthers), serenaded Arizona's governor, Phoenix, 1940.

Professional status, TWA, 1939.

managed to suck out a bunch of paper lunch boxes and anything else in the rear that wasn't fastened down. Even Sammy's skirt was being pulled into the abyss.

Fortunately there was an emergency button in the rear of the cabin intended to signal the cockpit. As soon as the door sprung open, Sammy hit the emergency button. When nothing happened, she hit it again. With a lone woman passenger in the rear looking on in great fear, Sammy pushed the button a third and fourth time. No response.

With concern only for her passengers and the safety of the airplane, Sammy decided she had to take action. The flight, from San Francisco to Boulder City, Nevada, included a striking view of the Grand Canyon from about eight thousand feet–*below* the open door. Sammy was not impressed. With adrenalin flowing and evidencing that mysterious super strength of heroism, she reached out into the slipstream, grabbed the handle and pulled the door back into place. Making sure it was securely locked this time, she rushed forward to tell the cockpit crew what had happened.

They told her the emergency buzzer had never gone off in the cockpit. In awe of her heroics, they carefully landed in Boulder City *without further incident*, as they say in aviation parlance.

Caught up in the excitement and the relating of her airborne experiences, Sammy confided in her Waikiki Beach companion another incident on one of her flights. This time it was apparently heavy turbulence, causing some passengers to "fly out of their seats." As Marsha relates it, "I went up to the ceiling, then came down amidst a jumble of dishes, silverware and blankets. I was serving breakfast, so the dishes were filled with scrambled eggs. When I came down, the eggs flew all over, including under my flared skirt.

"When we were all collected and somewhat back to normal, one of the male passengers looked at me with scrambled eggs still running down my legs and said: 'I thought everyone was frightened, but not *that* frightened.'"

In her innocent naivete, Sammy related these two incidents to her beach companion. What she couldn't know was the young woman was a reporter for a Honolulu newspaper. She had a "behind-the-scenes" story. With the guile (and glee) of an aggressive reporter, she wrote about the incidents, documenting from "firsthand sources" the dangers of flying.

Not only did Sammy tell Earl Thacker about what happened, but she also related the situation to another friend she had met on the islands. Roy Howard, perhaps best known as the "Howard" portion of Scripps-Howard newspapers, was told about the inquiring reporter tale.

Sammy had met Howard and his wife, friends of Earl Thacker and his wife, when Thacker had taken her on sightseeing tours of Oahu.

By whatever powers Howard held over newspapers (Scripps-Howard at that time also owned International News Service), the young reporter's scoop was suppressed–much to Sammy Sampson's relief, since she was sure her time with TWA would be severely curtailed when the story appeared.

Sammy had been victim of the sometimes hidden risks of dealing with the media. Those early lessons proved valuable in later life, particularly when she founded and directed Academy Pacific to the school's ever-expanding role in travel education.

Sammy Sampson's "near-miss" with the potentially damaging TWA story hadn't dulled her public relations value to the airline. Following her exciting two weeks in Honolulu, TWA's public relations moguls decided they wanted her to stay *another* four weeks, since the publicity coming out of there was tremendous and the PR professionals saw nothing but further positive results. Sammy knew she had to get permission from her boss, the chief hostess.

Sammy Sampson, Phoenix, Arizona, DC-2, 1939. Note TWA The Lindbergh Line on door.

TWA's Sammy Sampson with American Legion delegation, Burbank, 1940.

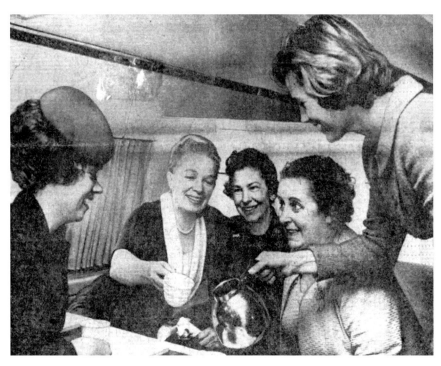

Los Angeles Times feature on three early flight attendants, 1965.

Alice Aldworth, Sammy Sampson (Marsha Toy), with photos in their TWA uniforms, 1987.

RIGHT PAGE: *Marsha Toy, the Hollywood glamour pix, 1950.*

When she wired her boss in Kansas City, the answer came back promptly. "No. Come back immediately."

However, that wire was superseded by another from TWA's president, Jack Frye, with a request that the airline would like her to stay another four weeks, all expenses paid, of course.

As a loyal employee, Sammy knew she'd have problems not only with the chief air hostess in Kansas City, but, nearer to home, with her immediate supervisor in San Francisco, Andy Andrews. Andrews, a retired TWA pilot, was in charge of all air crews flying out of San Francisco.

Employing all of her customer/passenger relations skills, upon her triumphal return to San Francisco she brought traditional Hawaiian flower leis. Sammy decided the best defense was a good offense.

She went directly from her disembarkation on the *Lurline* to the airport, climbed the metal stairs in the hangar to Andy Andrews' office, knocked quickly on the door, but went right in. She draped one lei around Andrews' neck, kissed him on the cheek and uttered a compelling "Aloha!" She did this a second and third time, each with a kiss on the cheek accompanied by "Aloha!"

In Andy's office was a salesman across the desk who could only remark: "God, what a job you've got!"

The extra four weeks in Hawaii were never again mentioned. Sammy Sampson was always treated well by Andy Andrews. Her chief hostess was in Kansas City, so she was miles removed from the action.

Sammy's friendship with Roy Howard and his wife that had begun in Hawaii led to a continuing relationship that sometimes took her to the couple's New York apartment. During one of her visits there, Roy Howard was interrupted during dinner by a phone call. As Marsha tells it, she overheard him saying: "I told you not to do that. It was absolutely the wrong thing to do. We talked about that and you said you wouldn't do that." After further irritated words, Howard told his caller they'd have to regroup and he would talk to him later.

When Roy Howard returned to the table, obviously agitated, someone asked him "What's the matter?"

Howard replied: "That was Wendell and he's going to lose the election."

The Wendell, of course, was Willkie, running for the U.S. presidency against Roosevelt in 1940.

It was another lesson for the young girl from Wilkinsburg: The power and influence of the press, even at the highest echelons of government.

One suitor Sammy met during her TWA San Francisco days was Clarence Toy, a young realtor from Burlingame, California (a San Francisco community where many air hostesses lived). Sammy and Clarence eventually became engaged–but not before some exciting adventures with other suitors.

On one flight as they landed, Sammy looked out the tiny door window of her DC-2. She spotted Clarence and another "boyfriend" awaiting her arrival. They were unaware of each others' presence or relationship to Sammy. Following the traditional "smile and goodbyes" at the rear door, Sammy stayed inside, quickly buttoned up the door, went forward to the cockpit and said, "Take me to the barn,

LEFT PAGE: ***Marsha Toy, head clinician, Bergstrom Army Air Field, 1942.***

boys. I'm not sticking my head out there." So the pilots turned the plane around and taxied into (well, maybe just to the front door) of the hangar.

Sammy and the crew deplaned, one of the pilots drove her home, leaving Clarence and the other suitor "waiting at the gate," so to speak.

Despite her near-miss with another young man, Sammy and Clarence were married June 14, 1941. That meant the end of her three-year flying career with TWA since rules in those days called for automatic separation for air hostesses/flight attendants who married.

The fates that brought her to California, her adventures in Hawaii as *Miss Aviation*, her exposure to top brass at TWA and Scripps-Howard and her marriage were remarkable, but there was one more twist.

A regular passenger on her San Francisco flights had been Tommy Hull, who owned, among other things, the St. Francis Hotel in San Francisco, another hotel in Sacramento, El Rancho Vegas in Las Vegas and the Hollywood Roosevelt Hotel in Los Angeles.

Although she didn't know it at the time, Marsha Sampson Toy's future path was already being charted in 1941.

As a wedding present, Tommy Hull hosted Sammy Sampson and her new husband at his El Rancho Vegas resort. Although El Rancho had all the Las Vegas niceties, including swimming pool, it was well before the incursion of the gambling influences of Bugsy Segal and others who pioneered flamboyant casino palaces.

Following an idyllic Las Vegas honeymoon, Marsha Sampson Toy and Clarence Toy were caught up in world realities of 1941. The *Winds of War* were blowing.

A Stanford graduate, following Pearl Harbor in early 1942 Clarence was given an Army Air Corps commission and assigned as a personnel officer on the staff that would create and activate Bergstrom Army Air Base in Austin, Texas.

Although she was no longer a TWA employee, Marsha retained her nursing skills. She was named the *civilian* nurse in charge of the clinic at the air base for more than six hundred civilian men and women workers building Bergstrom. The clinic included examining rooms and even an office for Marsha. She was the solitary clinician, so she had to not only minister to accidents, but to try to teach on-the-job safety. Despite her earlier protestations about not being a teacher, Marsha Toy began her *school days*.

Dressed in a white, starched uniform, complete with blue cape, Marsha treated women whose hair had been caught in revolving machinery, men whose fingers had been cut off by saws (even including one man who came to her first with two fingers severed, was healed and returned to work only to saw off two other fingers) and even visited homes of workers who had called in sick. Much to her surprise, Marsha found a few malingerers at homes she visited.

In one of her first supervisory jobs, Marsha was made safety officer for the construction crews. She walked the shop, spotting unsafe practices.

As an Army Air Corps officer's wife and as safety officer for the base, Marsha and Clarence were a part of the social whirl surrounding all these newcomers thrown together under wartime conditions. With the assignment of a new commanding officer, the staff held a welcoming celebration. When the general greeted Marsha in the receiving line, she let loose with some newly-acquired Texas-isms. She gave him a hearty, loud "Howdy Doodie." The general loved it.

Fun and games, Halloween party, Hollywood, 1952; Marsha Toy is in adagio costume on back of couch.

As were most senior air corps officers in those days, the general was a pilot. He offered to teach Marsha the skills of flying at a little, private field on the outskirts of Austin. The young nurse from Wilkinsburg, already practicing her supervisory and teaching skills, was introduced to the romance of piloting an airplane.

When Clarence Toy was sent overseas, Marsha returned for a short time to Pittsburgh, but came back to Austin when she heard Jackie Cochran was organizing what would become the Womens Airforce Service Pilots (WASPs) to ferry military aircraft to bases, both domestic and overseas. She saw an ad in an Austin newspaper offering flying lessons at Haile Field, near Austin. Marsha knew she had to get her pilot's license to qualify. She signed up with Doc Haile, taking beginners lessons (she had been given some basics by the air corps general) in Doc Haile's

Aeronca Chief, with its side-by-side cockpit that gave fledgling flyers more confidence. From his little hangar with its other small airplanes and a gaggle of airplane parts, Doc held forth with his potpourri of students, including playing poker with the troops.

When she logged her first forty-five hours of flight time, Marsha began to press Doc for lessons in aerobatics, which she *really* wanted to conquer.

To make sure she understood fully the rigors of aerobatics, Doc invited her on one flight (he was piloting) that began with his "knifing" between two trees, diving on his own hangar, then climbing to altitude where he rolled the airplane and flew inverted. Marsha recalled, "I was hanging upside down. Oil was pouring down in front of me in the biplane. I knew he was trying to scare me and I made up my mind he wouldn't do that. So I turned around to him (he was flying from the rear), hung onto the shoulder strap, waved and smiled. I thought if I acted scared, he'll never quit."

After they landed, Doc Haile was apparently convinced of Marsha's confidence and derring do. He had previously been convinced of her routine flying skills. He simply turned over the plane to her, walked away and said, "Go fly it!" A good psychologist, Doc never looked back.

Marsha decided if all those TWA pilots could fly one of these things, she surely could, too. She started the engine, taxied to the grass strip, revved it up, pulled back on the throttle and found herself aloft. "It was so thrilling and invigorating. I just wanted to keep on going up further and further."

She even learned to fly around pylons as well as performing stalls and spins at altitude. She had soloed, even descended while doing four spins. It was time to apply to the WASPs. Just after she completed her WASP entry physical, Marsha received a wire that Clarence was being returned to the States because he had a hernia. That ended her WASP saga since she knew Clarence would require an operation and she would have to nurse him back to health.

But one more piloting adventure remained. When Clarence returned to Austin, for their third anniversary in 1944, Marsha told him she had a surprise for him. She took him to Haile Airport, got him strapped into an airplane, then climbed in beside him. Clarence kept looking around for the pilot who would take them aloft. Marsha, who still didn't have a license, shared her conspiracy with Doc Haile, asking him to turn his back while she took off with Clarence as her passenger.

Marsha recalls: "I thought it would be wonderful. He'd get a big kick out of it."

Marsha circled the airport. She asked if he'd mind if they did a spin? Clarence was "frightened to death." His answer was a resounding "NO!" She thought he was going to have a heart attack, which could prove even worse than the hernia. When they finally returned to Mother Earth, Clarence, not the least bit impressed or amused, said "Never again!" That was their first and last time flying together.

Another incident that Marsha says today demonstrated that there are varying degrees of flying skill was her experience with Art Nelson, a TWA copilot whom she knew from her air hostess days in San Francisco. Nelson came through Austin and she asked him up for flight. Reaching altitude, she observed to Nelson that she felt so comfortable with him up there. If anything happened, she believed he could take care of everything.

Nelson's response was "Are you kidding? I wouldn't have any idea how to fly this thing."

Following the end of World War II, Clarence received Army Air Corps orders to report to Los Angeles as personnel officer in charge at the office there. Postwar housing was almost impossible to get. After spending days pounding the pavement, Marsha's friendship with Tommy Hull once again bore fruit. The Toys lived temporarily at Hull's Hollywood Roosevelt Hotel. Moreover, the friendship they had struck up with the commanding general at Bergstrom got them an apartment. The landlady of one apartment building and her husband were good friends of the general. Following hours of reminiscing, Marsha and Clarence had themselves an apartment in Hollywood.

That location would prove prescient in Marsha Toy's career as an educator with close ties to the aviation world. ✈

Marsha Toy Air Hostess School graduate on first flight, 1949.

THREE

A School is Born—in Hollywood

*"He that traveleth into a country before he hath some entrance
into the language, goeth to school, and not to travel."*

Francis Bacon

CLARENCE TOY WAS GAINFULLY EMPLOYED, GOING TO WORK EVERY DAY. Marsha wasn't, and didn't. She was bored. Her life in wartime Austin, Texas, had been exciting and glamorous: Head nurse and safety officer at Bergstrom Army Air Base. Wife of an officer on staff. Flying lessons.

Here she was in what was known worldwide as glamorous Hollywood, California, about which songs were written and where a movie star could be found around every corner or a soon-to-be discovered *ingenue* on every drug store stool. Despite the storied glamour of Hollywood, she was bored!

However, at least one incident sharply broke that boredom as well as providing Marsha with watermark opportunities for crisis management, press relations and human compassion. Their Hollywood apartment connections and Clarence's Army Air Corps personnel duties enabled them to meet Dick Bong, WWII fighter pilot and America's leading ace in the Pacific theater. The Toys became friends with the Bongs when they were able to get Marge and Dick Bong an apartment in their coveted Hollywood building.

Unfortunately, Dick Bong was killed in a test flight. On Marsha's shoulders—as the Bong's closest friends in California—fell responsibilities for handling press relations surrounding the death of one of America's war heroes, for consoling and even "hiding" his widow, Marge, and ultimately for accompanying the body and Marge to their home near Superior, Wisconsin.

Even today, nearly fifty years later, Marsha says she will always remember the sometimes bizarre events surrounding Dick Bong's death, his widow's grief and the task of making arrangements as well as consoling his father in Wisconsin.

Later, walking near that famed corner, Hollywood and Vine (a location that would play a major role in Marsha Toy's educational career), she saw a sign: *AIR-PORT GROUND SCHOOL.*

"Maybe I'll keep up with my flying and take some ground school training," she mused. Marching in, she told the people behind the desk she wanted to enroll. She related her background–nurse, air hostess, safety officer, flying lessons. With these varied credentials, the management of the Ground School envisioned a *jewel in the rough* whom they could add to their staff, attracting even more of the discharged servicemen who were flocking to schools nationwide under the GI Bill.

Marsha Toy accompanies widow of WWII ace Richard Bong in return to Wisconsin, 1945.

In her first formal exposure to organized education, Marsha became an instructor teaching people to work as airline reservationists and counter agents. As the school and its enrollment grew, she was named director of training. She even hired instructors. There were eleven on the staff. Marsha's job was to plan and write lessons designed, as she said later, "to keep ahead of the students."

However, Marsha's innate honesty and principles she learned at home in Wilkinsburg began to make her uncomfortable with the claims and commitments made by the school's management. She was aware of promises made she knew would never come to fruition. Too many applicants were being accepted and

Graduates ready for duty, Marsha Toy Air Hostess School, 1950.

steered into courses Marsha knew they could never successfully complete. She was fielding what she knew were legitimate complaints from students. She found that applicants were accepted who, even after schooling, could not be placed. Another responsibility given Marsha was placement director. She found that placing "graduates" of the school was almost impossible.

Marsha went to her bosses with a list of things she knew needed to be fixed. She was assured on two different occasions that all of her list would be addressed. To assuage her, they twice raised her salary. But nothing else positive happened.

The third time around Marsha announced she was resigning. She said she didn't want another salary raise. She recognized that practices she considered "shady" were <u>not</u> going to change. She gave them two week's notice, trained her replacement and left.

Out of work and once again finding herself bored with inactivity, Marsha Toy decided on another approach to education. It was her first venture into academia where she had a share of the ownership.

This time she, along with two others who had left the staff of the Airport Ground School (which had changed its name to California Air College), decided on a home study course for airline reservationists and ticket sales people as well as air hostesses–all subjects she was familiar with and had written many lesson plans around.

Marsha envisioned prospects not only for home study, but as an adjunct to women's grooming schools that were springing up all over the country. She visited thirteen U.S. cities in less than a month, presenting the merits of adding air hostess, reservation and ticket agent training to the curriculum of established grooming schools. Several of the schools signed up, but only one–in New York– stayed the course, so to speak.

Ill health of one of her partners, lack of interest from another and insufficient business from mail order and the New York school contributed to the demise of the home study school. Each of the three partners took a set of lesson plans. The partnership was dissolved.

By this time Clarence Toy had been discharged from the Army Air Force. He started his own business in San Jose. Marsha elected to stay in the Los Angeles area, continuing her pursuit of travel industry education. The industry was booming and Marsha correctly perceived significant opportunity. Most important, she realized that educating young people, preparing them for lifetime careers, was something she truly enjoyed.

Air Hostess School graduates with United DC-3, Burbank, 1950.

She and Clarence divorced.

With her home study partnership and her marriage both dissolved, Marsha had to decide where to go from there.

The School expanded, reception lobby, West 6th St., Los Angeles, 1967.

That decision was not a difficult one. By this time she knew she loved teaching young people. Why not teach them what she knew best? Air hostess!

Marsha was well aware postwar air travel was a burgeoning business. She believed airlines would be hiring all types of personnel. Air hostesses/flight attendants would be in demand. Her combination of talents–nursing, air hostess, safety instruction and specialty education–served her well.

However, knowing the airline business well, Marsha recognized that if she began a resident school for flight attendants, she wanted it to be under the aegis of a major airline. And, of course, the one she knew best was TWA.

She took off for Kansas City and a meeting with her former boss, Cliff Mutchler, who was by then the airline's operations chief, reporting directly to Jack Frye, TWA's president.

Mutchler encouraged her, but laid down a list of conditions to be met: her school must be established; the curriculum set; a skeleton staff in place; and satisfactory administration, screening and student follow-up. When these conditions were met, Mutchler said they would send a team of investigators who would vote whether the school could be affiliated with TWA and meet the airline's standards. If it met these criteria, the airline would give it a seal of approval.

Thus was the Marsha Toy Air Hostess School, precursor of Academy Pacific Travel College, founded in 1948. The McConnell School, Minneapolis; the Ward School in New England; and the Marsha Toy School in Los Angeles were the only three schools accepted by TWA. To be a TWA flight attendant, applicants were referred to one of these schools, expected to graduate and be hired by the airline.

All systems were "go." Marsha needed only a place to locate her school.

Van Nuys Airport branch, 1971.

As Meredith Wilson later wrote in *The Music Man*, "You Gotta Know The Territory!" Marsha certainly knew Hollywood and environs. She remembered her old friend Tommy Hull, who, among other properties, owned the Hollywood Roosevelt Hotel, a landmark and Southern California gathering place located prominently on Hollywood Boulevard. Just as he had with the El Rancho Vegas honeymoon, Tommy once again came through.

"Why don't you just use space on our Mezzanine. I won't charge you any rent because the space is only good for offices, anyway. And, you are not planning to have that many students so your needs are small," Tommy told Marsha.

"Oh fine. All I need are a room, some chairs and a blackboard," Marsha responded.

"You've got 'em."

In October 1948, six girls made up the first class of the Marsha Toy Air Hostess School on the mezzanine of the Hollywood Roosevelt Hotel.

This was the Hollywood Roosevelt Hotel of legend; the seat of old movie industry power; site of the first Academy Awards ceremony; crash pad for Marilyn Monroe; drinking haven for Errol Flynn; a room where Montgomery Clift later stayed (now reported to be haunted); location for film shooting that portrayed the glamour of Hollywood.

As appealing as it was, however, the Hollywood Roosevelt Hotel presented a problem. The classes were held in the evening to the accompaniment of rumba drums and music emanating from the world renowned Cinegrill right off the

Class room (or Telex), South Broadway, Los Angeles, 1960.

lobby. The first six graduates of the school were not only trained in the amenities of being flight attendants, but could move up and down the aisle of their airplane to a rumba beat.

The entire graduating class went to work for TWA—as did other classes for the next several years. The school's reputation was growing across the country and particularly in Kansas City. The only problem was that it's financial challenges were growing at the same pace.

"It took me only five years to lose every dime I had," Marsha lamented in 1995. At $150 per student and with a strictly-controlled six to ten students per class, the money was *not* rolling in.

"We were getting as many as 250 candidates a month, but we only enrolled a handful because we were so strict in our requirements." Praise was heaped on the school from TWA. Its nationwide reputation as the leader among the three TWA schools was well-deserved because the school graduated what were termed the "finest products."

First male graduate Doug Barr, diploma, 1954.

Not unlike today's Academy Pacific, the 1948-49 Marsha Toy Air Hostess School had strict admission requirements—and a commensurate high placement rate.

The foundation for today's Academy Pacific was carefully and solidly laid in Hollywood, California. Word spread of the strict admission policies, the dedication of staff (albeit a small one), and the high standards of the curriculum. Other airlines—Pan American, Frontier, Bonanza—approached the school about training their flight attendants. Moreover, other companies in the travel business queried about training people in reservations and ticket sales. The travel industry, freight business and airlines were all growing. The school grew in lock-step with its customers.

But financial strength was not in concert with business growth.

Marsha Toy thought expenses might be less in downtown Los Angeles than in Hollywood. Moreover, a major attraction was the opportunity (created when Marsha Toy went to them with an offer they couldn't refuse) to share space with well-known, reputable Sawyer Business College.

Marsha cut a deal with Sawyer for rental of a classroom and associated services and, if any of her students evidenced interest in office or secretarial training, she would send them to Sawyer.

Thus, in 1953 when her students stepped off an elevator on the seventh floor at 7th and Broadway in downtown Los Angeles, they were greeted by the sight of hundreds of other students busily heading for classes. Although the Marsha Toy Air Hostess School had only about six students at the time, the Sawyer enrollment made it look like more. The atmosphere at the schools was electric.

Applicants for the Air Hostess school lined the extra chairs placed in the hallway awaiting interviews. Concurrently, the financial picture began to improve. The only *external* funding aid for students came from the GI Bill, however. For the most

Doug Barr, awaiting boarding, PanAm Boeing Stratocruiser, Honolulu International Airport, 1956.

part, students paid in cash but they needed to have available some form of short-term financing.

That led to another step in Marsha Toy's creative thinking process.

She marched across 7th Street to the Bank of America branch office and put forth her proposal to the branch manager. She explained about the school, her students needs for loans and the financial viability of the whole venture. But, she added, the school also needed to be refinanced with a loan.

With classic banker's caution, he asked what equity she could provide.

"I have a car," she told him.

"Fine. Get your car, drive by and I'll stand outside and look at it." Marsha's financing plan was approved.

It was only later, however, that the allegedly-conservative banker confided in her that when he saw her drive by (with appropriate hauteur) in her old jalopy, he knew he was in trouble. He had to hide her approved loan papers in the bottom drawer of his desk. But she received her $5,000 loan. And, she directed students who needed financial aid across the street to the Bank of America branch.

With the newly-infused $5,000 working capital, the school began to grow in every way: enrollment, curriculum, and reputation.

CAEA Certificate of Merit for Outstanding Curriculum, 1956.

Professional staff, Airline Schools Pacific, 1955; Marsha Toy front right.

In effect, the school was guaranteeing the student loans with Bank of America as well as doing referral and solicitation work for BofA. When Seaboard Finance Corporation heard about this business, they took initiative to make a business proposal to Mrs. Toy. It was infinitely better than BofA's deal, so she grabbed it,

School and attendance growth continued unabated, causing Marsha Toy to wonder to herself: "Why not set up our own finance company that will not only make it easier for our students but, in addition, the interest revenue will come to us instead of some external company?"

Thus was created American Student Loan Association, an in-house finance company established solely to grant student loans to Airline Schools Pacific (the new name for the school) enrollees. With separate offices and a staff of three, business boomed.

The growth of the school (enrollment was now at about four hundred) and the success of the finance company caused the school to expand, taking over the entire seventh floor of the building at 7th and Broadway in downtown Los Angeles.

In addition to air hostesses, by 1956 the curriculum included reservations, ticket sales, air freight and travel agency duties. But, of course, Airline Schools Pacific's interest and dedication were still to the airlines. So another move was

Working class rooms, South Flower St., Los Angeles, 1968.

Class room, Computer Training Center, South Flower St., Los Angeles, 1968.

made. This time to newer, more modern quarters on the second floor of a building on 6th Street in downtown Los Angeles, in the heart of the airline offices that were then mostly on or around 6th Street. The school and the American Student Loan Association were both flourishing.

However, in 1968 the U.S. government stepped in with the Federal Insured Student Loan Program. With an easy-to-acquire down payment of only about fifty dollars and a payback six months after graduation, the Feds loan program was much more attractive. The in-house American Student Loan Association was no longer needed. What *was* needed, however, was a bank to handle the federal loan. Marsha cut a deal with the downtown branch of Wells Fargo.

Although she recognized that the federal student loans could provide a helping hand for her students, Marsha nonetheless resented the federal intrusion. "I didn't want the government to have any part in running my school."

Travel Show exhibit, Academy Pacific, 1969.

AP graduate Ed Weigandt, TWA Flight Attendant, 1951.

President Of Airline Schools Visits Islands

By MARY COOKE

Trim and slim and looking like the airline hostess she once was is Marsha Toy, president of Airline Schools Pacific, Inc. in California.

She's not only its president, but also its founder.

She's the girl who, in 14 years, has taken it from its beginnings as an air-hostess training program to a travel business school that teaches travel agency management, reservations and ticket sales, a full secretarial course, an air-hostess course and languages.

This month she added an English course for foreign speaking students, explaining that the schools get several foreign students a month.

"We even have an office in Hong Kong now," she said. "One of our former students, a Chinese boy, interviews and reviews applications for student visa entries.

"AND DON'T think I'm not giving some thought to Honolulu. I've been reading

MARSHA TOY

the papers and visiting facilities to see what the potential might be for setting up a school here."

Miss Toy arrived last week for the Airport Operators Council meetings and will vacation on the Neighbor Islands until Sept. 1 when she returns to her home in Hollywood Hills.

SHE SAYS she maintains her office at home and "moves around to the schools" which are in Los Angeles, Santa Monica and Long Beach. Students range from high school age to about 40, and 80 per cent of the enrollment now is men.

She says students not only receive placement in the travel industry when they graduate, but get temporary jobs to help defray tuition and living expenses while they are studying.

"We have one staff member who does nothing but handle temporary job placement for students," she said.

MISS TOY began her career as a registered nurse, then became an air hostess for TWA.

"In those days air hostesses had to be nurses," she pointed out.

Twenty-three years ago she made a trip to Hawaii as "Miss Aviation," and later, in 1948, she began an air hostess school to train stewardesses for TWA and Western Airlines. After five years she began offering the courses from which her present schools grew.

Triumphal return to Hawaii, Honolulu Star-Bulletin & Advertiser, 1962.

But federal student loan programs, now the most common form of financing for all types of advanced education, had their start in 1968. Banks loved them. Still do. But enrolling students and arranging for their financing took on a different outlook.

All that stirring up of enrollment and financing was also reflected in other school business. Booming enrollment and more classes brought another move: this one to two full floors in a building at 737 South Flower Street in downtown Los Angeles. Moreover, with strong impetus from her admissions staff, Marsha Toy opened a series of satellite admissions offices–Long Beach, Santa Ana, Van Nuys, Santa Monica, Covina. With the influx of candidates at these outlying offices, the natural progression was to open a classroom with instructor at these locations. Ultimately, there were fourteen locations for Airline Schools Pacific, from Washington, D.C., Honolulu, Seattle, San Francisco, Oakland, San Bernardino, Santa Barbara, Oxnard, and including downtown Los Angeles.

The rapid expansion, including financing of the physical plant necessary for the schools to meet the strict standards laid down by Marsha Toy caused a financial crisis–including an embezzlement of $300,000.

Determined not to file for bankruptcy, Marsha Toy drastically changed not only the way her school was administered and financed but her own living style as well. With a determined effort to save the home she owned in Hollywood, she rented it out and moved into a small, lower level guest room where she lived for five years while, in her own words, she "worked harder than ever and kept praying."

The perseverance paid off (as ultimately were all outstanding debts). "When I realized what I had to do, I never felt bad. I just kept working, seven days a week, and I managed to pay off all the bills."

At the Itchy Scratchy _Hotel, Molokai, Hawaii, 1962._

There was even a Small Business Administration loan of $75,000, which–true to AP standards and practices–was repaid on time. In fact, the repayment of this SBA loan was a success story duly reported by the media.

With the 1971-72 turnaround in school fortunes, Marsha Toy decided it was time for yet another move — this time to Hollywood Boulevard and Gower. All debts were ultimately paid off, enrollment was growing, the school was profitable.

"I heaved a big sigh of relief. I felt so good I decided to have my office painted, with the painter coming in on a Sunday to do the job," she recalls.

"I had a call at home on Sunday morning from the painter who told me he couldn't paint there."

"For heavens sake, why not?"

"The building is on fire!" he replied.

Dressed only in nightgown and robe, Marsha rushed to the scene and found firefighters battling flames from windows and doors. They extinguished it, but offices and classrooms of Airline Schools Pacific were destroyed. Seems a taxi com-

Los Angeles

Times

PART V ★

FRIDAY, DECEMBER 22, 1967

A Mother Hen to Stewardess Chicks

BY JEAN MURPHY
Times Staff Writer

It's easy for a woman to succeed in her own business without really trying. The only requirements are intelligence, acumen, talent, energy and guts. Good looks and charm can help, too.

Observation and induction indicate that Marsha Toy, founder, president and owner of Airline Schools Pacific, possesses all these qualities. The only characteristic she will admit to having, however, is energy.

"In the early days, I used to leave the office at 4 a.m. and start work all over again at 9 a.m. And I kept that schedule for quite a few years," she recalled.

The "early days" were back in the 1940s, when the young ex-hostess opened a school for stewardesses. She began with eight students, a contract from Trans World Airlines and a room in the Hollywood Roosevelt. Today her organization consists of seven schools with 38 full-time employes and 28 part-time teachers; it will graduate about 400 students this year and gross more than $1 million next year.

The main school, 14 rooms of offices and classrooms, is located in downtown Los Angeles at 532 W.

6th St. The other schools, which operate under franchise, are in Long Beach, Santa Ana, Covina, Van Nuys, Santa Monica and Oxnard.

Miss Toy, a vital, vivid woman, casually attributes her success to a "Topsy" growth.

"I have never reached out agressively to do any of these things," she said. "I've never had a long-range goal and I don't now."

That her schools will continue to grow seems inevitable. "More people want to franchise schools than I have time to talk to," she said. "My philosophy is not to expand rapidly; I have to be very careful to protect the ethics of the organization."

In addition to hard work, Miss Toy believes women must be tenacious if they are to succeed in business. "You've just got to grit your teeth and hang on."

Being a woman is not really a disadvantage, she has found.

"In the beginning, it was difficult. I always felt men were patting me on the head, were patronizing me, but it's not that way any more. I really think a woman has a better chance to succeed in business than a man . . . you're remembered just

Please Turn to Page 3, Col. 1

SUCCESS STORY—Marsha Toy, right, president and owner of Airline Schools Pacific, encourages Usha Sukhita, student from India.
Times photo by Mary Frampton

because you are a woman."

As a young woman from Pittsburgh, before the thought of business had ever entered her blond head, Marsha Toy was a TWA stewardess with an RN pin on her uniform and two boyfriends in every port. After three years of traveling in DC2s, she was grounded by marriage. It was after her marriage ended in divorce that she opened her school for stewardesses.

More Men

Nowadays, Airline Schools Pacific trains comparatively few stewardesses because the major airlines provide their own training. Men students predominate in a curriculum which includes such courses as reservations and ticketing, operations — communications, air freight and cargo sales and service, travel agency work, languages and business skills.

"Of course, we can't guarantee jobs but we do

place 97% of our graduates," said Miss Toy. After 20 years in the business, she still sounds a little suprised at her own success.

"When I was young, I only wanted one thing—to be married and have six children. I didn't approve of career women," she smiled wryly. "I really have a feeling for young people. I guess that's why I'm in the school business."

Even in 1967 she was the "Mother Hen," Los Angeles Times.

Commercial Schools Offer Wide Subject Matter Variety

Placement on Jobs Is Major Goal

BY DEWEY LINZE

There are a few professions in the world which lack textbooks, but if all the textbooks used in Southern California in the study of professional trades, businesses and hobbies in nontax supported schools were piled into a mountain, there probably would be a textbook to be found to tell how to climb to the top.

In the Southern California area, there are more than 300 commercial schools which teach a variety of subjects from embalming to modeling and which are attended by students who have not yet reached their teens to others who can hardly remember them.

Investment of proprietors in these schools is in the millions of dollars. Many of the schools are operated under the watchful eye of the examining boards of the state; others have regular city business licenses.

The only guarantee that these commercial schools offer, not unlike any public school of tax subsidy, is that they will teach the subjects they advertise. There is, of course, a matter of quality in the instructors, and there is the receptiveness of the student to consider.

BBB on Guard

The Better Business Bureau is on guard against unscrupulous schools. It has quite a file on schools which have been the targets of complaining students who didn't seem to come away with what they paid for.

TOUR HANGERS—Don Jackson, center, shows students from Airline Schools Pacific, Inc., a passenger service unit used in American Airlines jet. Marsha Toy, far left, president and founder of the school, watches during the tour.
Times photo

OUTLOOK PROFILE

Wartime Copy Girl Turns Into National Public Relations Firm

BY NORRIS LEAP

During World War II's manpower shortage when a Times deskman or reporter yelled "Boy!" a pleasing minor miracle would occur. There materialized instantly at his elbow a girl. Usually she was young, usually she was lovely enough to worry Miss America.

energy nor of ability that got her "fired." It was the ending of campaigns for which she'd been hired.

Joblessness was merely a challenge. She took on the editing of a little weekly publication here, then of another and another.

Finally she was editing 12. But anyone who knows how much work there is in

Recognition of "Commercial Schools," including Academy Pacific, Los Angeles Times, 1961.

American Aviation

JANUARY 20, 1969

TRAINING

Airline Schools Pacific Trains 3,000 Yearly

Is there a shortage of employment opportunity in aviation?

Not according to Marsha Toy, vivacious president of a rapidly growing network of educational institutions known as Airline Schools Pacific.

At least 97% of the 3,000 students her schools turn out this year will have been placed in employment the moment they graduate, and she claims that she could just as easily place 30,000 a year.

Granted, the aviation employment outlook may not be that bright throughout the industry. Positions as airline captains, airport managers, executive pilots, vice presidents and chairmen of the board will always find more applicants than vacancies. But Miss Toy's philosophy is that those opportunities present themselves more readily to the person who already is in the industry than to one who is on the outside looking in.

That is the precept upon which she has expanded a business from a parlor operation 21 years ago to a multiple-location undertaking now conducted in 13 facilities, from Honolulu to Washington, D.C. By the close of 1969, there may be twice that number of Airline Schools Pacific, operating in New York, Chicago, Miami, Dallas, Atlanta, Boston, and possibly even in London and Tokyo.

Secrets to the runaway success of Marsha Toy and Airline Schools Pacific appear to be twofold. First, her program is designed to provide fully trained personnel in areas of activity in which the airlines and associated industries do not provide training programs themselves. Second, a placement service is operated to provide employment for graduates with airlines, travel agencies, freight and air cargo companies throughout the world.

AMERICAN AVIATION, JANUARY 20, 1969

The standard curriculum for all Airline Schools Pacific reflects to a degree the occupational areas in which graduates are placed. Included in the 730 hours of classroom work are courses in flight procedures, international travel, reservations and sales, tariff regulations, typing, ticketing, airline space control, routes and codes, Teletype operations, government flight control, airline safety procedures, communications, sales techniques and languages.

Miss Toy found herself in the aviation education business when, after leaving her job as a stewardess with Trans World Airlines, she was retained by the company to school other young hostesses. Today, because virtually all of the major airlines provide their own stewardess training programs, fewer than 5% of Airline Schools Pacific graduates go into that line of endeavor.

Convinced that there was an unfilled training need, however, Miss Toy went to the personnel managers of all airline and related companies. Slowly she began to devise a curriculum to prepare

youngsters for hard-to-fill positions or those in which employers experienced a heavy need. From the first facility in Los Angeles, Airline Schools Pacific branched out to Santa Monica, Long Beach, Van Nuys, Covina, Santa Ana and Oxnard, all California, then to Honolulu. In 1968, additional schools were opened in Washington, D.C.; Seattle; Santa Barbara, Calif.; Riverside, Calif., and San Francisco.

The schools, which boast a 70% male enrollment, are approved by the U.S. Department of Health, Education and Welfare to participate in the federally insured student loan plan. They are approved for veterans training and for training of nonimmigrant alien students, and are accredited by state boards of education in the jurisdictions in which they operate.

Miss Toy, with her brothers, Stanley and Harold Sampson, initially developed the Airline Schools Pacific chain as a turnkey operation. After opening a new facility, they would sell it to a local manager under a franchise arrange-

Aviation trades chronicled the School, American Aviation, 1969.

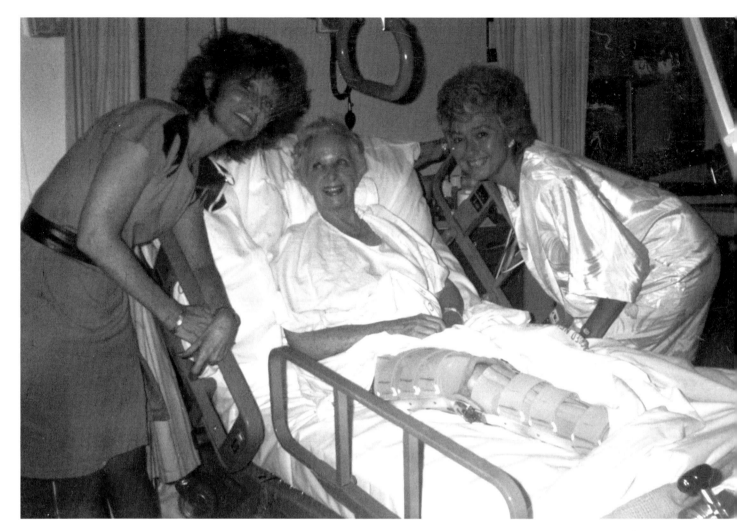

Hit and run victim, Cedars Sinai Hospital, 1989.

RIGHT PAGE: **The famed Hollywood Roosevelt Hotel.**

pany next door had been burgled the night before; the burglar set fire to the place to cover his unlawful act.

Just as her school had regained its former stature, had gotten out from under a heavy financial burden and enrollments were increasing, Marsha Toy recognized there was no way the charred location could be salvaged.

Only six weeks later, after an exhaustive search for suitable quarters, the school once again relocated. This time, Marsha Toy and her school planted her flag at one of the most famous intersections in the *world!* In 1978 the school established a beachhead on half-a-floor in the Equitable Building at *Hollywood and Vine.* It was only a few blocks west of the fire-scarred class rooms and offices that had been home for Airline Schools Pacific for several years.

A four-floor-high sign, *ACADEMY PACIFIC,* still towers above that legendary corner, although the school moved from there in 1988.

The growth and progress during those halcyon years dictated a name change, evoking the continually broadening nature of the school. From *Airline Schools Pacific* it became *Academy Pacific Travel College.* It better reflected the school's expansion.

"We started with half of one floor and ended up with one full floor ... eleven classrooms ... with between three hundred and four hundred students," Mrs. Toy fondly recalls.

Even with the glamour of its Hollywood and Vine location, Academy Pacific was pushing at the walls of its quarters. They obviously needed more space.

With the business acumen and dedication that marked the forty year history of her schools, Marsha Toy took another bold step to ensure the continuing success of her efforts. She bought a building!

Two blocks north of the former location (and that famous sign at the corner of Hollywood and Vine), the building is Academy Pacific's present location at 1777 North Vine, Hollywood — directly across the street from the famous round-like-a-stack-of-records Capitol Records building in Hollywood.

This wasn't just *any* building. It would fit the school's needs but Marsha knew they needed two full floors and probably part of a third. There were tenants in the building that had to be politely and gently (as only Marsha Toy could achieve) moved out to make way for Academy Pacific. That process took more than six months to accomplish; ample time for Marsha to design *exactly* what she knew from more than forty years of running a school would work.

"I drew plans exactly as I wanted. I was so intrigued by this opportunity to start from scratch and do just what I knew would succeed that one weekend I went for two full days drawing plans to scale. I forgot to eat. But when I was finished I knew what we had would work. It's pretty much what we have today."

Everything seemed to be going along swimmingly. "I thought I could sit back and relax a bit.

"Then I got hit by the car!"

Ironically, Marsha had just come from visiting a friend in Cedars Sinai Hospital in Los Angeles. It was March 24, 1989. She was heading for dinner at a Sunset Boulevard restaurant. Parking her car in front of the restaurant, Marsha got out on the driver's side to lock it when she heard the crunching sound of metal on metal and the "thwonk" of metal on skin and bones. It was a hit and run.

If the old axiom that "bad news come in threes" is true, Marsha Toy had *exceeded* her quota: 1) The loss of her startup funds; 2) The financial crisis of the '60s; 3) The fire in the '80s—and now this!

The next thing she knew, Marsha, only half conscious, was being wrapped in coats and blankets—with uniformed policemen leaning over asking her name–in the middle of Sunset Boulevard in preparation for the ambulance trip as an emergency room patient right back to the hospital she had just come from as a visitor.

At the feisty age of 74, Marsha was taken to the Emergency Room (well before it became the popular ER TV show) with a dislocated shoulder, a compound fracture of the right femur (thigh) plus fractured tibia and fibula (lower leg bones) on the right leg, a deep gash on her left leg, and severe head and face trauma. As she was being treated in the ER, Marsha recalls the doctor who kept coming in to check on her. "I could tell from the expression on his face that he didn't give me much chance."

But as the team continued to treat her (including with shots of morphine so they could reset her shoulder), Marsha recalls making up her mind through the haze, shots and frantic pace of the ER that she was going to make it. "I don't know how I knew, but I just knew!"

Later in the operating room, they installed a metal shaft in her right leg as well as a couple of large screws to hold her together. "I still have trouble at airport security checkpoints because of all that metal that's still there."

A young resident kept coming in to visit her, check her vitals and all the things busy doctors do in hospitals. He told her later he was always surprised by how well her vital signs read and by her amazing progress.

"I just want to tell you something. I know I'm going to get better. I don't know how I know, but I know," she told the young physician. He was convinced Marsha's attitude, in fact, aided her recovery.

That positive outlook rubbed off even on the psychiatrist who came around, probing about her attitude, the accident and the driver. "I'm not angry at the man who hit me. That's his problem, not mine. I feel fine and I'm sure I'll come out of this OK." The young psychiatrist was so impressed she began relating some of her own problems to Marsha.

Hospitalized for a month together with several months of therapy and care at home, in August 1989, Marsha returned in a wheelchair, then later on crutches to direct the activities of Academy Pacific.

"We were well-staffed ... our school was in good condition ... but our overall financial picture for that year wasn't as bright as I'd like to see it. I recognized we needed strengthening at the top ... the administration. So, I began to take steps to fix that."

Evidence that Marsha Toy had succeeded in infusing Academy Pacific with her own strengths came as the school entered the decade of the 1990s with a wide divergence of curricula to meet the changing needs of the travel industry. ✈

CUNARD WHITE STAR
THE UNITED STATES & CANADA
LINK WITH THE EAST COAST AND
THE CONTINENT
L. N. E. R.

FOUR

TRAVEL IS SERVED

"To be really cosmopolitan, a man must be at home even in his own country."
Thomas Wentworth Higginson

ALTHOUGH ACADEMY PACIFIC SCHOOLS HAD GONE THROUGH SEVERAL generations since its founding in 1948, its period of greatest growth, stability and expansion came in the late 1980s and the 1990s, when founder Marsha Toy returned with a vigor from her near-fatal accident.

In the 1960s had come a geographic expansion with fourteen locations from Long Beach and Santa Monica to San Francisco, Santa Barbara and San Diego. The web stretched as far west as Honolulu (there were obviously sentimental ties from the days of *Miss Aviation*) and to the east as far as the nation's capital, Washington. As evidence that this expansion was not accomplished simply to flex the schools' corporate muscles, more than half of these *off-site* campuses were accredited by the National Association of Trade and Technical Schools—a mark of recognition with significant meaning to students and employers alike.

However, the establishment of Academy Pacific in its own 45,000-square-foot building in 1989—not far from the school's original location—provided permanent roots. Three floors of the building are now dedicated to classrooms, workshop laboratories, and administration, all with functional objectives—just as Marsha Toy envisioned them.

With the wisdom of perspective gained from forty one years (at that time) in business, Marsha Toy had elected to return Academy Pacific close to its original home—in the heart of what had been perceived as the glamour capital of the world, Hollywood. The purchase of the building on Vine was visible evidence of Marsha Toy's confidence in not only the potential for Academy Pacific, but for the restoration and resuscitation of Hollywood itself. The area had fallen on hard times in the decades of the 1970s and 1980s. Hollywood had lost much of its glitter. Looking beyond the tackiness of those less-than-glamorous times, the school, along with other businesses and individuals who had confidence in the future of what had once been known as *Hollywoodland*, made financial commitments to help assure

LEFT PAGE: ***Some of the tools of travel, Cunard White Star, 1925.***

Tim Ho, Los Angeles Mayor Sam Yorty, at "neighbors" ceremony, Honolulu airport, 1962.

the continuation and importance of that magic name.   In a mid-1990s major feature, the *Los Angeles Times* noted, "After decades of being treated as the region's outcast, historic Hollywood may be on the verge of a rebound that could make it the most effective symbol of Southern California's urban renaissance."

Academy Pacific — and Marsha Toy — had bet its future on that urban renaissance.

Moreover, the boom in the travel and hospitality industry made Academy Pacific graduates even more marketable. The curricula now included Reservations, Ticket Sales, Travel Agency, Cruise Lines, Amtrak, Hotels and Restaurants as well as English as a Second Language and remedial courses (tied to hospitality and travel).

From its modest beginnings as an *air hostess* school, AP curriculum expanded exponentially to meet the job requirements of the industry it now served as a unique educational resource.

For example, a cornerstone of AP's curriculum is its Transportation Management: Customer Service program. Tailored to meet travel/reservations/hotel agent needs (travel agent, tour operator, ticket agent, air operations, passenger service agent, reservations agent, sales representative, hotel front desk, service staff), training is job-oriented and practical.

Included in AP's 750-hour Transportation Management curricula are such subjects as Speech/Communications, Travel Marketing, Physical Geography, Travel

Agency Theory, Ocean and Cruise, Rail and Car Rental Marketing, Customer Service, Hospitality, Increasing Human Effectiveness and more than fifteen other courses designed to graduate travel and tourism professionals.

Retaining its link to the 1948 Air Hostess beginnings, Academy Pacific continues what is today known as Flight Attendant (eliminating any gender identification or prejudice) training.

"Many U.S. and international airlines don't do their own flight attendant training. They look to us because they know we have a nearly fifty-year record of providing top quality cabin personnel," observed Marsha Toy.

Many courses in this 750-hour Flight Attendant program are common with others at the school, but more than one hundred clock hours are devoted exclusively to Flight Attendant training. One course common to all AP curricula is Career Development, specifically designed by school administrators to guide students into long term careers in the travel and tourism industry, one of the largest businesses in the United States.

The society column, Airport Operators Council; Honolulu Star-Bulletin, 1962.

Famed Metropolitan Opera tenor Lauritz Melchior, Honolulu, 1964.

Although all AP vocational classes are conducted in English, a major program at the school is English as a Second Language (ESL). Convinced that foreign born or intermediate English proficiency students should not let English interfere with their job career plans, AP offers levels of ESL classes, from Intermediate to Advanced.

Making an education in travel and business particularly appealing and attractive to Southern California's growing ethnic minorities, Academy Pacific offered opportunities for hands-on, practical training.

Academy Pacific installed different travel and tour computer systems (including four created by major carriers): American, Delta, United, Northwest, TWA, and Texas Air/EDS for airline reservations plus one for hotels that is, appropriately named MARSHA (for Marriott Hotel computer system). The airline reservation computer programs are SABRE, APOLLO, WORLDSPAN, and SYSTEM ONE. These programs, taught at AP, are universal throughout the world travel industry. The school is electronically linked to a computer focal point that keeps its own systems updated with each change.

In addition to basic programs, including essential computer skills, Academy Pacific offers elective courses for professional advancement to include advanced computer programs as well as a remedial program focusing on skills needed to function successfully in society. Remedial courses are offered in such subjects as mathematics, social studies, writing skills, essay, science, interpreting literature, plus the arts and reading comprehension.

In its modern, five-story Hollywood facilities, AP classrooms include an aircraft mockup as well as state-of-the-art audio visual equipment, telephone training equipment, travel lab and individual computer reservation terminals. In addition, the school has is own library as well as student and faculty lounge areas plus student dining facilities. Assuring the most focused personal attention, classrooms are designed to accommodate as few as fifteen students, but no more than thirty. In concert with most modern educational institutions, AP provides letter grades as well as grade point average (GPA).

Maintaining high standards of acceptance and academic excellence prevalent since the school's founding, students must have a GPA of at least 2.0 to graduate. Those with a GPA of 3.75 (4.0 is highest) or higher are listed on the school's Honor Roll. Their diplomas record the honor.

In one very striking—and visible—example, AP is unlike many other educational institutions: STUDENT APPEARANCE! A walk though the halls and classrooms is eye opening.

Convinced that Academy Pacific students are in training to work in locations and environments that encourage (even require) proper professional attire, AP has stringent dress codes. Students and staff alike adhere to dress codes that include dark skirts for women; slacks for men; white blouses or shirts; blue blazers as appropriate and school-provided, unique-design scarves for women and ties for men. In addition, there are strict rules about hair grooming, shoes, hose/socks and overall appearance. Students in Flight Attendant programs must adhere to height/weight restrictions. They're weighed weekly.

Projecting a unique concept that students (whether young people or mature adults) achieve better in a regulated environment (and with recognition that the industry they are training to serve expects well-groomed individuals) Academy

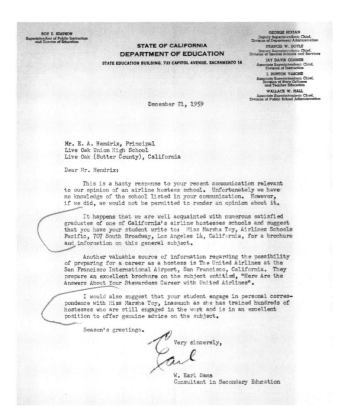

Strong reference from California Department of Education, 1959.

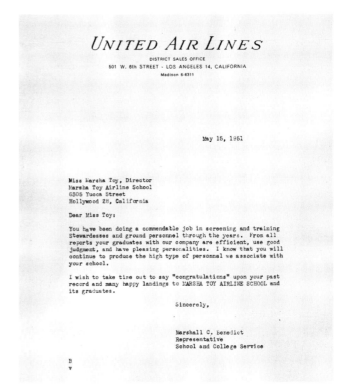

Support from United Air Lines for the Marsha Toy School, 1951.

Recommendations from former employer, TWA, 1955.

Pacific has consistently held high standards for dress, behavior, attendance, attitude and, in today's environment, absence of substance abuse. Applicants are carefully and selectively screened at the outset of their interest in the school. Then, upon acceptance, they are continually evaluated on not only academic aptitude, but appearance and attitude as well. The school makes it clear that failure to meet its standards in any of the three "A's" (academic, appearance, attitude) are considered grounds for dismissal. Moreover, students are informed that "Any student who is dismissed because of conduct detrimental to the best interest of the College or student body will not be reinstated."

"If they object to the rules that we impose, they have the option of going elsewhere for their education," opines school founder Marsha Toy.

An intriguing aspect of this "tough love" concept is that it works! The school has graduated more than 25,000 individuals. The current placement rate (the percentage of graduates who are placed in full-time positions) is slightly more than 87 percent. That means nearly nine of ten graduates are employed within a week to four months of their graduation.

One major attraction for AP students and graduates alike is the school's continuing career guarantee that

THE WINNER—For the ninth year Academy Pacific awarded a full-tuition Transportation Career Scholarship as part of 1981 Air Youth Day, sponsored by the California Aerospace Education Association. Here, Catherine Calamia of Edgewood High School, West Covina accepts this scholarship from Marsha Toy, president of the school.

FOREIGN STUDENTS AT ACADEMY PACIFIC

Strangers in a strange land are made welcome at Academy Pacific, where approximately 10 percent of the student body comes from overseas.

Among the countries represented in the school's international roster are Germany, Greece, Japan, Mexico, Nigeria, the Philippines, Romania, Taiwan and Thailand.

Many foreign students enroll at Academy Pacific to learn the skills of the travel industry with plans of returning to their native countries to seek employment.

In the countries where interest in Academy Pacific runs high, particularly Japan, Thailand and the Philippines, the school has official representatives to counsel and assist prospective students with the necessary paperwork for the student's visa.

Students make their applications by mail, and upon acceptance, student visas are processed.

All students applying to Academy Pacific, whether foreign or from the United States, are administered an in-depth interview, as well as a standard Otis aptitude test.

The aptitude test, conducted fully in English, is considered necessary because it provides some indication of linguistic level as well as ability to qualify for training.

If the foreign student scores low on the Otis test, he may take the Personal Development course, a computer program which builds speed and skill through repetition, at no charge. The school also offers a fluency course in English, also available at no charge.

GEOGRAPHY CLASS—Nigerian student Adeshola Oluwole Adehoyo, called "Wally" for obvious reasons, points out the location of Lagos, Nigeria, on the classroom map to fellow-student Roxana Quesada.

BERTHA & CARLOS RUBIO—Both students at Academy Pacific and the parents of a one-year-old son, look forward to furthering their respective travel careers. Carlos, born in Cuba, was an electrical engineering student at the University of Havana when he decided to immigrate to the U.S. in 1966. He lived in Chicago until 1975, when he moved to Los Angeles, where he met and married Bertha. Here, Carlos discusses a point in the tariff with Bertha during the computer class.

The School's current campus building, Vine Street, Hollywood.

LEFT PAGE: *Evidence of the United Nations Look at AP, 1981.*

they may revisit classes at any time for updating or skills improvement. This guarantee is at no additional cost to the student or graduate.

The career guarantee is particularly appropriate for computer reservations systems where data is sometimes changed daily to reflect fare adjustments or schedule changes.

However, this career guarantee extends not only to computers skills but to all aspects of an AP education. Staff members who serve as tutors for students follow individual progress. If they are aware of enrollees who aren't quite up to speed on a particular subject, these tutors work with students on an individual basis. In addition, students absent because of illness or personal home problems are individually tutored, at school or even at home via telephone if the situation demands it, until they are caught up on class work.

With its metamorphosis into a full-schedule travel school, Academy Pacific made certain its class schedule met the needs of working adults as well as traditional daytime students. For example, many students (and instructors) are "in classrooms" as early as 6:30 in the morning. Night classes begin at 5:30 p.m. and dedicated students are often found in the laboratory classrooms well after 10:30 in the evening.

Water ditching drills for flight attendant students, 1996.

English As A Second Language (ESL) class, Hollywood, 1989.

RIGHT PAGE: *The many faces of AP, at locations, 1995.*

AP students are frequently "on location," 1996.

To assure that its program is open to all, AP classes are held year round with closure only on the traditional holidays.

With its expanded educational scope AP's "front office" operations were, of necessity, also expanded.

Initial exposure for potential students is the Admissions Department that provides preliminary screening of applicants. Students must have a high school diploma or equivalent before graduating. In addition, applicants are screened for character, personality and normal physical health. Each applicant is given an Ability-to-Benefit test as well as evaluated for remedial education. Applicants who make it through the stringent initial screening of the Admissions Department consider themselves part of an elite group who have passed through their first tough wickets.

Academy Pacific is a strong advocate of equal opportunity. Walking through its halls, classrooms and at its graduation ceremonies provides clear evidence of this concept. Students and families of every race, creed and color are present.

The Placement Department has enjoyed significant success, but the school makes it very clear it "does not guarantee employment or obligate itself beyond reasonable assistance and guidance." Placement service is available to all AP graduates qualified for employment in the facet of the industry for which they trained.

Although the school was a pioneer in student loans and financing, modern-day complexities have made it imperative to offer a Financial Aid Department that guides students in financial aid programs under the broad headings of grant and loan assistance. These include such Federal programs as Pell and Federal Supplemental Educational Opportunity Grants as well as Federal GSL, Perkins, SLS and PLUS loan assistance programs. With its wealth of experience in student financing, the AP Financial Aid Department is of substantial help to students who are often confused and unsure of what they can apply for — or what to expect. Moreover, experience of staffers is a boost to students. Victor Lintong on the financial staff, for example, has been with the school for seventeen years.

Academy Pacific has been recognized by the National Association of Trade and Technical Schools and the Career College Association for innovative ideas (such as the tutorial program).

"We encourage schools all over the country to do the same thing. It saves a lot of dropouts. It's a *win-win* situation for everyone," notes Marsha Toy. Remaining active in all aspects of education, she has served on the Board of Directors of the National Association of Trade and Technical Schools, frequently exchanging ideas and concepts with other school principals.

As AP's curriculum and student body enrollment increased when the newly-acquired building and its specially-designed classrooms became fully operational, the challenge of additional professional staffing with administrative and teaching personnel became an imperative.

"It seems there are people who know how to administer and others who want to nurture and who enjoy dealing with young people, but you must find just the right combination of those interests," says Toy. She noted the difficulty of combining these characteristics.

"The individual must have a nurturing, caring, feeling about young people. Second, they have to know how to manage a staff. Finally, they have to know how to make the 'bottom line' pay off," she added.

One longtime staffer was also the first male graduate of what was then the "air hostess-oriented" Airline Schools Pacific. Douglas J. Barr, now AP's Director of Public Relations, originated many of the school's innovative programs. As he put it, "I was impressed with Marsha Toy's enthusiasm and her aura of success."

Barr enrolled in AP, graduating in 1953.

With valuable experience working in the travel industry, Barr later returned to the school, became an instructor and subsequently moved into administration and management, ultimately becoming the school's spokesman.

Recognizing the value of spirit and incentive, Barr in 1988 began what has become one of AP's most coveted and inspirational programs, the Excitement Team (popularly known as ET). Over its eight-year existence ET has evolved as a group

Marsha Toy, Founder/Director,
with Doug Barr, 1st male graduate,
Public Relations Director, 1995.

Excitement Team, ASTA TravelFest '95, Queen Mary,
Long Beach, 1995.

of highly-motivated student volunteers who instill spirit, responsibility, leadership, and self-confidence into the student body and the school.

In addition to serving as a motivational and rallying organization, ET members work as volunteers at industry trade shows; help plan travel seminar and tours to airports, cruise ships, hotels, resorts and travel agencies; serve on AP's "Graduation Committee," including such graduation-related activities as the Valedictorian Breakfast and Alpha Beta Kappa (honorary travel society) activities; host special events on campus such as International Day; and, of most significance to the "outside" world of community relations, supports orphans at the Hollygrove Children's Home plus serving as monitors and fund raisers for PBS/KCET television's periodic pledge breaks.

As one facet of its ongoing commitment to prepare AP students for the business world, in early 1996 ET members participated in five different travel shows as customer service representatives. They had the opportunity to mingle and work with travel pros and consumers alike. ET members receive credit hours for their volunteer work. In addition to hands on experience, ET volunteers were participants at large area travel shows and guests at industry hospitality events at the Regent Beverly Wilshire and Red Lion hotels.

In 1991, ET was recognized by National Association of Trade and Technical Schools for Best New Department.

In addition to his creation of inspirational programs, Barr writes and publishes a periodic newsletter for students and alumni. He also creates and distributes AP news releases and arranges for tours and hands-on visits to area travel venues. Barr continues to do some teaching, including classes on parliamentary procedure (for example, how to run a meeting).

Despite the euphoria over its own unique facilities as well as an expanding curricula and student enrollment, one facet of America's education movement concerned Marsha Toy.

With particular emphasis on proprietary schools such as Academy Pacific, she became increasingly concerned with government involvement in the financial aspects — loans, grants and even curriculum standards. In addition, the Pennsylvania street kid who set high standards became increasingly aware of less-than-honest school operators who were apparently taking advantage of and manipulating the government's involvement in education. A scandal resulted from this "manipulation" and there was plenty of finger-pointing to go around. The result, as is often the case when the Congress becomes involved with special issues, were tougher laws and regulations governing proprietary schools. Are the schools better off as a result? Possibly not, but most proprietary school officials agree this federal oversight is one price paid for a representative/participatory form of government.

As Academy Pacific headed into the decade of the 1990s and ultimately into the twenty-first century in its own facilities, Marsha Toy was convinced the school's leadership was well-balanced, structured to meet the expanding needs of students as well as the economy and the demands imposed by an increasingly complex world. ✈

AP graduate Maria Nunez. other AP graduates, Valedictorian Breakfast,
Hollywood Roosevelt, 1995.

※ Five ※

Travel Prospects

"It is right to prefer our own country to all others, because we are children and citizens before we can be travelers or philosophers."

George Santayana

"WHEN MORE RIGID GOVERNMENT EDUCATION REGULATIONS WERE IM-posed in 1989, the entire industry—career schools and colleges of technology—was better off as a result," according to Dan Gilreath, Academy Pacific's chief compliance officer and fourteen-year veteran of the school's staff. "So-called 'marginal' schools simply couldn't measure up," he said.

"But the new regulations had minimal impact on Academy Pacific because we were already meeting all requirements," Gilreath added. With quiet modesty reflecting his long-time loyalty to the school, Gilreath said, "We're the best."

Everyone on the staff of more than forty-five professionals seems imbued with the philosophy of being "the best." Pride of the staff is evident—even palpable—on the urban campus. Professionalism, adherence to dress code, cleanliness, an upbeat attitude are all descriptions that characterize the people who run the school. This attitude—and projection— of the professional staff is reflected in the student body.

Academy Pacific is a fully accredited school by the Accrediting Commission of Career Schools and Colleges of Technology (ACCSCT). That translates to recognition by the U.S. Office of Education and the Department of Education. Not only does this rank Academy Pacific among the top-rated career colleges, it enables the school to receive Federal funds in order that students may be eligible for federal education grants and loans. Trained professionals are available to enrolling and continuing students for guidance on what type of financial aid is available. Gilreath notes that the process for handling student financial assistance (including federal loans) has been made much more prompt and efficient because of computers.

Gilreath's admittedly biased view is understandable. With more than 100,000 graduates since the school was founded in 1948, scores of AP alumni have distinguished themselves in the travel and tourism industry.

Cynthia Ann Rodriguez, AP graduate, member of the school's Hall of Fame and Certified Travel Consultant, is currently Los Angeles representative for the Cayman Islands Department of Tourism. "The foundation and basic travel/tourism education

I received at Academy Pacific enabled me to move immediately into the travel industry," she said. "I had confidence in my own ability because I knew I'd taken courses necessary for my professional career choice," Rodriguez added.

In 1994, for example, 285 students graduated from Academy Pacific. Of graduates available for immediate placement, 82 percent went to work in the hospitality and travel industry. An even higher rate–97 percent of the Flight Attendant program–were employed in their chosen profession. Academy Pacific flight attendant training (with its roots going all the way back to Marsha Sampson Toy's 1938 TWA service as well as her original school concept in 1948) is recognized for its high quality. In addition to AP graduates in flight attendant service with a wide range of medium and small airlines worldwide, several major U.S. carriers hire AP flight attendant graduates, complementing their own internal training schools.

United and American, for example, have a number of AP flight attendant program graduates in service. Smaller carriers, who do not have internal training programs, utilize a high percentage of AP graduates.

One organizational technique to assure that AP maintains its "best" rating (as well as to make certain the school is current in its curricula) is the Travel Industry Advisory Board (TIAB). Created several years ago, TIAB is comprised entirely of outside travel and tourism professionals who serve voluntarily, meet quarterly and whose recommendations are taken seriously at Academy Pacific.

One TIAB member (general manager of the Burbank Airport Hilton and Convention Center) recently observed, "Although I sit on many travel industry boards, no group better represents a cross section of the travel industry than Academy Pacific's TIAB group." He added: "The caliber of individuals who participate on the board is first rate. Not only does each industry professional attend quarterly meetings, but each person actively supports the student body by providing field trips, coordinating industry career days and making guest lecture presentations."

Evidencing the close liaison with students, this TIAB member noted: "The student and TIAB are given every opportunity to spend as much time with each other as possible to ensure students' understanding of the travel industry. TIAB is involved in almost all special education and motivational events that take place on and off campus."

Because of TIAB and continuing AP special event programs that provide students with "hands on" experience at travel shows, airport tours, internships, airline and cruise ship tours, tourism promotions and "front counter" opportunities, the school has close relationships with companies serving the industry. This not only pays off in student experience during their school days, but it also helps AP's placement professionals find career opportunities for graduates.

For example, AP graduates have been placed with airlines ranging from American and Aero Mexico to United, USAir and Virgin Atlantic. Graduates can be found at large, medium and small travel agencies ranging from American Express to Mexico Travel Advisors. The hotel and resort industry, from Marriott to Hilton to Sheraton to Ramada, have scores of AP graduates.

Tour operators and packagers such as Club Med, Pleasant Hawaiian Holidays, Jetset Tours, Heli LA, and Nature Encounters, Ltd. as well as freight companies including FedEx, AMR Services, Ogden Allied and Gateway Freight all boast

Academy Pacific graduates on their professional staffs.

Railroads–Amtrak, BritRail, French National and Via Rail Canada–together with cruise lines such as Norwegian, Princess, Galaxy and Royal Caribbean all employ AP graduates.

Car rental companies, including Alamo, Avis, Budget, Dollar, Hertz, National, all include AP graduates on their staffs. A Budget Rent A Car executive, a member of the school's TIAB, said she "found my participation within the council both trying and exhilarating.....a relationship with which the Academy and I grow.....together!" This Budget executive commended the establishment of TIAB as a way "to create closer rapport with the companies and suppliers who hire from America's first travel college."

Leaders in the travel and tourism industry who are employers of AP-trained graduates are high in their praise of skills taught at the school and the caliber of those who come from the Hollywood campus.

"....the College's number one focus is its students. Their standards are high and they are constantly upgrading their curriculum to keep abreast with changes made in the vast and growing industry," said an executive with the United States Virgin Islands Division of Tourism. She continued, "The entire administrative team is very professional...a definite role model for each student because future employers will look at a well-rounded student when choosing candidates for employment."

First AP Hall of Fame inductees, Pamela Rentz, Cheryl Durazzo, Janet Kahle, with Marsha Toy, 1988.

Marsha Toy conducts staff seminar, AP conference room, 1995.

A Malaysia Airlines executive who frequently is a guest lecturer at Academy Pacific took particular note of appearance and attitude. "The classroom is always attentive. The students are always well dressed and on time for my presentations." This airline executive says Academy Pacific has an industry-wide reputation for "dedication to education."

The fastest growing element of the travel market is "ecotravel." It is defined as sustainable travel (that is, travel that relies only on available natural facilities), including in small groups in order not to disturb fragile ecosystems; contributing to local conservation efforts; and benefiting natives as a result of visits by the group. A partner of Nature Encounters, Ltd. is a member of AP's TIAB. Evidencing the wide diversity of the school's travel interests and curriculum, the Nature Encounters partner says, "Academy Pacific should be commended for bringing every aspect of the travel industry into their classrooms and, in this way, their students graduate fully prepared to enter the travel world."

AP staff at Graduation ceremonies, 1992.

TIAB member Philip Westernoff, South African Airways, provides first hand experience, 1996.

Providing visible evidence of support for AP, the Nature Encounters partner was a participant in—and provided inspiration for—a 1996 Academy Pacific graduating class.

The Western Regional Manager for South African Airways notes: "... the college has made a commitment to the future of its students and takes very seriously its role and responsibility in maintaining a high profile within the Southern California travel industry." A member of the school's TIAB, the South African Airways executive states that he is "...a proponent of our educational institutions and private industry working together to the betterment of our future."

Further testimonial to AP's professionalism comes from the District Manager for the Bahamas Tourism Center. She says, "...graduates of Academy Pacific....possess a high level of education as well as on-the-job experience and exposure." Moreover, she observed, "The curriculum and equipment will satisfy the job training needs of employees in the labor market."

A former QANTAS executive (no longer in the travel industry) recalls that the airline always counted on AP graduates for top employees. "We knew if they graduated from Academy Pacific they would be excellent employees."

A recently inaugurated AP program is "Education Plus," a series of one-hour travel and tourism seminars that offer students an in-depth study into such categories as Transportation, Destination, and Hotels and Resorts. The seminars are led by members of TIAB, who provide personal experience in each of the categories. Each of the seminars targets a specific mode of transportation, a particular destination, whether large or small, or the intimate details of the handling of guests at a world-renowned, designated hotel or resort.

At periodic Education Plus seminars, students are encouraged to participate in discussions, asking questions and learning firsthand from knowledgeable, professional seminar leaders.

National Car Rental, one of many AP graduate employers, LAX, 1993.

One student, an emigre from a middle Eastern nation, effuses about her experience at the school. "We're like a family .... like home ... even like your parents," she said. "I know that everyone at Academy Pacific–from Mrs. Toy through the entire staff –*cares* about the students." This student's praise for Marsha Toy is almost boundless. "The school is the way it is because of her. She keeps track of everybody. For Mrs. Toy, the school is love ... it is a part of her," the student observed.

Another AP graduate, out of school for eight years and now a travel industry executive, put it succinctly, "I am what I am because of Academy Pacific and Mrs. Toy."

Every member of the AP staff, including Mrs. Toy, proudly wears a big, colorful button reading, "STUDENTS COME FIRST!"

Despite Marsha Toy's regular, daily interest in the school's activities, she is *not* a micro-manager. Within the broad guidelines for the school's policies and codes, curriculum, and administration,

AP students at MGM Grand Air exhibit, National Business Travel Association, Los Angeles, 1994.

each staff member is given broad ranging responsibilities for their own area. Individual directors, respectfully loyal to Mrs. Toy, are given free reign to pursue areas of special interest and expertise.

As evidence of dedication to the concept that "the student is No. 1," AP several years ago started a tutoring department. Open to everyone, tutors are available from 7 in the morning to 7 at night. For entrants from other nations, part of the regular AP curricula are English as a Second Language (ESL) classes. Because of the emphasis on English in the travel and tourism industry (for example, English is the universal language for pilots communicating with air traffic controllers in towers the world over), AP makes certain its graduates are proficient in English in their chosen field before they enter the work force.

Along with the highest admission standards, Academy Pacific's educational program and curriculum are tailored to meet exacting standards in the industry. The Director of Training says "the curriculum covers ... the basic areas of travel: airlines, travel agencies, ground services, tours and cruises. It's reinforced with worldwide geography, both physical and travel destinations."

AP students are "on stage" for Hong Kong Tourist Association at Travel Spectacular, Universal Citywalk, 1996.

Founder/Director Toy addresses Valedictorian Breakfast, Hollywood Roosevelt, 1995.

AP booth, Travel Show, Los Angeles, 1995.

The seven-and-a-half month, five hour/five day-a-week program is tailored to meet weekly objectives on subjects students will encounter under actual job conditions. Most students take all classes in their chosen speciality; those who need extra, catch-up coursework take ESL and GED (General Educational Development certificate in lieu of high school diploma) classes.

The school has a cadre of professionals with extensive experience. For example, Kathy Miller, an education department head, has been with the school for twelve years. Another education department head, Steve Price, is a ten-year AP veteran.

A major advantage of a small school is knowing individual enrollees.

Classes are small enough (average less than fifteen students per class) and total admissions per session are sharply limited so that each student can have the "luxury" of a personal counselor on the staff who tracks that student's performance and progress through his or her entire enrollment. The counselor monitors attendance, academics and compliance with dress and behavioral codes.

Members of the professional staff discuss parental involvement in the student's training. Recognizing that parental attention is not possible in all cases, staffers often serve as "stand in" family, providing guidance, advice and counsel and sometimes simply serving as a "sounding board."

The staff stresses the personal attention provided each student, including discussion and suggestions for improvement during weekly staff meetings. If a student is evidencing a problem–either academic or personal (that impacts on attendance or attention)–the student's problem is discussed among the staff to determine whether it is unique to a particular class subject or is affecting that student's overall performance. Whatever the conclusion, the personal counselor – with suggestions from other staff members – assumes the responsibility for resolving or alleviating the problem.

A program unique to Academy Pacific is "custom tutoring" – designed specifically for students who, after enrolling, find they have limited time availability.

Leonid Karpovich, AP graduate from Russia, tells of his ESL skills at graduation, 1993.

AP English As A Second Language (ESL) class, 1995.

International Day at AP with costumes and cuisine; LAX tour, United Airlines, LAX, 1995.

Open only to students who have been trying and who evidence a positive attitude, custom tutoring can frequently rescue a student with great potential but whose personal situation might otherwise have caused them to be a dropout.

The ethnic mix at the school reflects that of the Southern California area, in particular. Gilreath notes that it has remained constant for the past 10 years. The ratio is: 50 percent Hispanic; 15 percent African American; 15 percent Asian; and 20 percent Anglo/Caucasian. Gender mix is 2/3 female and 1/3 male. Gilreath notes that Hispanics, who have the highest graduation rate of any ethnic group, also have a placement advantage because of language skills (Spanish and English). In today's global world, ability to communicate in more than one language is a definite plus.

The school's Director of Training is extremely sensitive to the wide range of career choices available to students as well as to their personal objectives. "We are not just an educational institution, but a *training* college. We must make sure our employer clients are served by trained, disciplined graduates. School philosophy, expressed to students early on, is: "You have made a decision to study here; you believe in yourself; stay focused; do your homework; you are investing in *your* business to get a return on your investment. Academy Pacific serves as a consultant to help you manage your time, your money and your career choice. You must be convinced that you have made the right decision."

The school's curriculum and its operating codes are designed to train students to deal with similar challenges they will face in life and in the workaday world. The professional staff works personally with students to make certain they are guided toward appropriate career choices and are trained to meet those choices.

AP's professional staff not only tracks students through their academic career but into their professional life as well. Through the school's Alumni Association graduates are followed during their working career—frequently challenging because of the fluid nature of the travel industry.

A basic tenet of Academy Pacific's student policy is what is often referred to as its "lifetime guarantee." Simply stated, the policy says that any AP graduate can return to the school at any time in their working career for refresher classes on subjects to help them update or learn new techniques to aid them in their job. At no cost. In other words, any time a gainfully employed graduate who feels a need for added training on a specific subject that student can return to AP for a new or refresher course—free! For example, many computer programs (APOLLO, SABRE, etc.) utilized by airlines and others are frequently changed or updated. If the employer themselves does not offer update training, Academy Pacific will.

A catch-slogan originated at Academy Pacific is *We Teach the World!* Makes a nice, memorable promotional slogan. The fact is, it's true!

The broad ethnicity and cultural diversity of the student body as well as subjects covered at what continues to be called "America's premier travel college," assure that Academy Pacific is truly global in perspective.

The theme of a 1996 graduation was *Welcome to Our World.* The graduation's pageant included students from Brazil, Chile, Indonesia as well as the United States. As these students moved through the audience they selected at random individuals who came forward with them and introduced themselves along with the students. The audience reflected the school's ethnic diversity with at least four different countries represented. An important element of this "audience participation" at graduation was the *pride* of families in their graduates. Family members were acknowledged and saluted by AP professional staffers who recognize what home encouragement can mean to students. Moreover, the *esprit de corps* evidenced by the professional AP staff, including rousing rounds of applause from the student body as the staff was introduced, made it clear that *Students* (do, in fact) *Come First!* ✈

A.P. students from around the world. Carla Kemp from Belize, Central America, Jessica Lee from South Korea, Geetha Warnasuriya from Sri Lanka, a colorful addition to Travel Spectacular '93.

Mixed ethnicity of AP students evident at ASTA Travel Spectacular, 1995.

AP students at Hong Kong "Wonders Never Cease" drama at Universal CityWalk, Los Angeles, 1996.

SIX

TRAVEL CAN BE GLAMOUROUS

"I am a citizen of the world."
Diogenes the Cynic

T HE STUDENTS . . . THE STAFF . . . THE DIRECTOR . . . ARE ALL DEDICATED to Academy Pacific as a professional travel and business college. But, make no mistake, the "glamour" of travel is an attraction for all.

Romantic destinations. Places in the world that many have never before seen. The glitter of ocean cruising. Historic venues that some have only *read* about. Jetting off to exotic locations. All combine under the broad heading, *The Glamour of Travel.*

One 1983 AP graduate, now working in marketing for the Department of Tourism, Cayman Islands, participated enthusiastically in a combined alumni gathering and Caribbean promotion. She commented: "It's my way of saying 'thank you' to the school that gave me my start in the travel industry." The gathering, held at a Marina del Rey hotel, featured food of the Caribbean, appropriate dress and music and what at least one attendee described as "just people, friends, sharing with others." With representation (many of whom were AP graduates) from such diverse interests as Burbank/Glendale Airport, Budget Rent A Car, Travel Advocates, British Airways and American Express, the informal dinner and entertainment was evidence of the ongoing spirit and enthusiasm of AP staff and graduates.

School alumni attending the event spoke glowingly of both their undergraduate work at AP and their subsequent experience in the industry.

"After I graduated I got a job with Continental Airlines, then traveled to many areas of the United States and the world, including Japan. I'm convinced that the people in our industry are dedicated to helping others," one graduate noted. He said, "I am so enthused about an AP education that I have a brother who is now studying at AP."

Note frequent use of the word "enthusiasm." With many AP staffers, the words "glamour" and "enthusiasm" are synonymous. Doug Barr says: "...because of the nature of the industry, it in itself generates a certain enthusiasm. I know when I go into a lecture about a destination I have experienced, I emote a lot of enthusiasm."

Thus, the obvious *enthusiasm* that is a part of the Academy Pacific culture— from the director through the staff, the instructors and onto the students—is a major facet of the *glamour* image that is associated with the travel, tourism and hospitality industry.

Despite that glamorous image, AP students toiling to make their eventual career choice whose faces glow brightly at graduation are faced with rigorous schedules — both day and night. For those students who are committed to daytime jobs, there are night classes running from 5:30 to 10:30 p.m., Monday through Friday. According to school records, about one-third of the enrollment is night students. The other two-thirds is scheduled for 7 a.m. to noon or 8 a.m. to 1 p.m., depending on class schedules. A high percentage of students are involved in other school activities after formal class hours.

Even with the potential glamour of travel and tourism dancing in their eyes, Academy Pacific candidates are quickly brought back to the reality of "nose to the grindstone" requirements when applying for admission.

Director of Admissions Sandi Dover, who oversees the entire process, underscores oft-stated requirements that applicants must have a high school diploma or obtain an equivalent GED on graduation; are given tests for English comprehension; must pass the Ability-to-Benefit test (judging the applicant's long-term potential); demonstrate a positive attitude; and evidence characteristics that are parallel to the school's high standards. Acknowledging that enrollment requirements and standards are extremely high, Dover says, "Our goal is to see that our students graduate and get placed." Noting that the industry is, for the most part, a person-to-person business where AP graduates are continuously exposed to the public, Dover observed that "our extremely high academic and dress codes—many call them *professional* standards—prepare our students for what it will be like in the real world."

Dover also notes that "there is no leeway" in entrance requirements; that means no "bending" the rules. The school and its students must meet all state and federal requirements. Although English comprehension is one of the tests given applicants, AP recognizes that it is often not an applicant's native language. English as Second

Brendan Tours guest speaker at AP classroom, demonstrating tour brochure, 1996.

Alpha Beta Kappa (ABK) inductees at Valedictorian Breakfast, Hollywood Roosevelt, 1995.

Language (ESL) classes offered at the school prepares students for being comfortable taking vocational courses which are all taught in English. Dover, herself a veteran at Academy Pacific, has Jennifere Clayton, a seven-year AP staffer as an important part of her team. Dover notes that AP students come from "all over the world," but English is the generally accepted language of the travel industry.

Newly-enrolled students are briefed by Doug Barr during their first week at AP. The role of the Excitement Team is outlined as "a way and means for them to participate in all the activities and events both on and off campus." The ET motto is "World friendship through education and understanding." The motivated volunteer students executes on and off campus efforts that provide experience resulting in leadership, self-confidence and self-esteem training as well as learning to take responsibility.

Credits for much-sought-after ET participation are accrued by students. ET members accumulate credits and move through several levels of recognition. The ultimate ET honor is a personally-engraved plaque presented at graduation. Most important, ET achievements are reflected on student's final resume so that potential employers are aware of this extracurricular activity. An interesting plus for ET par-

A.P. CRUISE DAY

Cruise Day for the students of America's First Travel College always attracts an enthusiastic and eager group.

In addition to classroom lecture and videos, A.P.'s customers participate in frequent visits to a variety of cruise ships docked at Los Angeles Harbor. Visits include an in-depth inspection tour, including passenger accommodations, lounges, library, casino, restaurants, gift shops and boutiques, swimming pools and gymnasiums, sun deck, lido, bars, theatres, hospital, etc.

A cruise line sales representative discusses 'sales techniques' and the shipboard amenities. From time to time, students have a chance to sample the gourmet cuisine on board, and are invited to lunch in one of the ships' dining-rooms. It's all a part of 'learning by doing.' A.P. thanks the following cruise lines for their continued support of America's First Travel College:

**CARNIVAL CRUISE LINES
CUNARD LINE, LTD.
NORWEGIAN CRUISE LINE
PRINCESS CRUISES
ROYAL CARIBBEAN CRUISE LINE**

Here we see students on board Norwegian Cruise Line's "Westward," docked at Los Angeles Harbor. The 28,000 ship is 674 feet in length, a passenger capacity of 829 with an international crew of 370. (Photos by A.P. Public Relations Dept., April 25, 1993).

ticipants is learning parliamentary procedure–how to run a meeting–a procedure many have never before experienced or even been exposed to.

The ET group is in evidence at graduations, tours, conventions, exhibits, seminars and other travel industry-related events where the AP volunteers help organizations achieve results while the ET group gains invaluable off campus experience. It's a "win/win" situation.

In addition to ET, another prestigious extracurricular activity is the campus Epsilon chapter of Alpha Beta Kappa, the National Honor Society in the arts, sciences, trades, business, technical and general studies. Purpose of the society is to encourage and recognize superior student achievement, character and leadership. ABK chapters are located in nationally-accredited institutions that have demonstrated high standards over a period of years in the education and training of men and women in a variety of fields, including trades and occupations essential to modern society.

AP students at lunch aboard Carnival Cruise Line Jubilee, Los Angeles Harbor, 1995.

Left Page: **AP "Cruise Day" aboard Norwegian Cruise Line's Westward, Los Angeles Harbor, 1993.**

Strict Alpha Beta Kappa acceptance criteria–including a 3.75 Grade Point Average (GPA), 90 percent attendance record, demonstration of leadership, participation in student activities–make the honor society a coveted (and elite) organization. Membership generally is confined to the top three percent of each class. The society's emblem is a gold key, presented at the school's graduation ceremonies. The class valedictorian is traditionally a member of Alpha Beta Kappa.

Networking in the travel and tourism industry is maintained on a continuing basis through the school staff's active association with three major industry associations: American Society of Travel Agents (ASTA); Pacific Asia Travel Association (PATA); and the Association for Promotion of Tourism to Africa (APTA).

Thus, not all work at AP is "nose-to-the-grindstone, dedicated classroom duties." Direct exposure to the "glamour" of the travel and tourism industry–and the fast-growing hospitality industry–is achieved through continuing tours and field trips to Southern California's wide range of venues as well as during in-house seminars plus hosting guest speakers from the industry.

In 1995-96 AP students toured such exciting locations as Los Angeles International Airport (LAX), Burbank Airport, the Regent Beverly-Wilshire Hotel, the Sheraton Grande Hotel in downtown Los Angeles, the ASTA Travel Spectacular, the Los Angeles Visitor and Convention Bureau's PowWow national meeting at the Los Angeles Convention Center. In addition, United Airlines Operations Department at LAX, hosted on-board tours of 747 aircraft. On the sea side, a specially-arranged full day aboard Carnival Cruise Line's luxury *Jubilee* cruise ship plus Cunard, Norwegian, Princess and Royal Caribbean cruise lines tours and briefings were arranged for AP students.

In addition to on-site seminars and tours of cruise lines, AP students are also given exposure to hotels and car rental procedures and techniques at actual locations.

On-campus seminars include such topics as *Springtime in the Rockies*, a VIA rail trip across Canada, car rental practices and procedures by National Car Rental, and a broad range of guest speakers from such diversified travel industry icons as Virgin Islands Division of Tourism, KLM Royal Dutch Airlines, Puerto Rico Tourism Commission, ITT Sheraton Hotels, Pasadena Travel Center and Hilton Hotels, including their Burbank Convention Center.

Off-campus activities for AP students serve a two-fold purpose. Students are exposed to hands on, reality-based training while prospective employers have the opportunity to observe AP students in action for future hiring consideration.

However, travel and tourism isn't all glamour . . . all fun and games. The industry is growing steadily despite some economic roadblocks in the United States in the early 1990s (drop in dollar exchange rates; typhoons in the East; earthquakes, fires in the West). According to the Travel Industry Association (TIA), tourists took more than 232 million trips to the United States in the summer of '96, a record number. Exceeding industry projections, it is a two percent jump over the summer of '95.

Travel and tourism is extremely important to California's economy. TIA says American travelers spent more money–$44 billion–in California in 1994 than in any other state. Florida was second in '94 with $29 billion spent by tourists. Of greatest interest to AP students and graduates is that TIA estimates travel spending in California supports 604,000 jobs in the Golden State. With downsizing of the state's aerospace and defense business, travel, tourism and the hospitality industry–always a strong player in California's lineup–has taken on even greater significance as an economic power hitter. Another California industry, entertainment, is linked closely with travel and tourism because it is a destination lure for travelers who flock to the

AP Flight Attendant students during tour of McDonnell Douglas American Airlines MD-80, Burbank Airport, 1996.

state to see firsthand the locations and people so often seen on television and at their local movie houses.

AP graduates who have distinguished themselves in the travel and tourism industry are accorded special recognition by election to the college's permanent Hall of Fame of travel industry professionals. Since the Hall of Fame's inception in 1987, six Academy Pacific graduates have achieved the prestigious recognition of selection for the school's Hall of Fame. Criteria for selection includes a "body of work" contributing to travel and tourism progress over an extended period of time; a leader-

AP students, including ET members, on location at Aero Club, Hong Kong Tourist Association, Pacific Asia Travel Association, Carnival Cruise, International Day at school, 1996.

AP students aboard Carnival Cruise Line's Jubilee, Los Angeles Harbor, 1995.

Flight Attendant students tour American Airlines MD-80, Burbank Airport, 1996.

AP tour of United Airlines Boeing 747-400, LAX, 1995.

Flight Attendant Students await arrival of incoming flight, Burbank Airport, 1996.

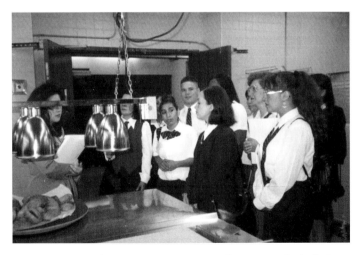

Hospitality Management students are briefed on kitchen operation, LAX Marriott Hotel, 1996.

Flight Attendant students are briefed at Caterair facilities, LAX. 1995.

***ET officers with Mexico Soccer team, Mann's Chinese Theater, Hollywood,
National Tourism Week, 1996.***

Kris Parker, Summer Class Valedictorian, graduation, 1993.

ship position with an industry-related organization; and a history of demonstrated contributions to progress and growth of not only the organization, but other individuals as well. Induction in the Hall of Fame is generally made during the school's graduation activities.

AP activities are chronicled on a regular basis by the school's Public Relations Department under the direction of Doug Barr. With each AP-associated participatory event, a news release goes to media describing what students are doing today. External communications, in addition to news releases, include the school's catalog and special newsletters to those in the industry with unique interests. And, of course, regular appearances of AP students at external events such as the KCET Public Television Pledge Programs assures visibility for the school and its student body.

Internally, AP students are exposed to two newsletters, one monthly and one annual summary. Encouraging communications and interaction among students, most participate in special events on campus such as International Day when students come to school in

AP staff and students at informal "get together," 1995.

the dress of their native land and bring cuisine from their country for a truly international buffet, complete with appropriate music. An annual picnic, a Holiday Festival, a Halloween pot luck are additional examples of school activities that encourage participation. Again, a two-fold purpose is served with these events: student interaction, being a part of the whole; and encouragement of gregarious contact that is a requirement for almost every job in the travel, tourism and hospitality industries.

AP staffers and instructors are regular participants in these special events, assuring a continuing flow of communications. As Doug Barr states, "Anyone who is not aware of what we do must have their head in the sand!"

Admissions Director Dover, sensitive to the mixed ethnicity of Academy Pacific's student body, observed that "Our college looks like the United Nations." She noted that the travel industry lends itself to a wide ranging ethnic mix. The student body trooping through the halls between classes and meeting in the all-purpose room, the special events and the graduation ceremonies reflect the broad ethnicity. Many proud families, attending ceremonies to see their loved ones graduate, also reflect the ethnic mix that is evident in both the travel industry and the California culture.

The glamourous attraction of travel is, like the siren songs of Lorelei, an attraction to potential Academy Pacificers. But, the reality of passing rigid enrollment requirements as well as high academic and dress standards established for the school, soon bring students a recognition of what's it's like in the real world. ✈

AP graduation gala, complete with caps and gowns, Hollywood Roosevelt Hotel, 1995.

A Reality Check for Graduates

"Modern air travel means less time spent in transit.
That time is now spent in transit lounges."
P. J. O'Rourke

SCHOOL DAYS OFTEN REFLECT THE INNOCENCE OF YOUTH: HIGH EXPEC- tations after graduation and the students' conception of protective armor often associated with academia. Moreover, at Academy Pacific the glamour of the travel, tourism and hospitality industries adds an even greater aura of what some critics of academia refer to as a fantasy world.

Graduation from Academy Pacific—complete with caps and gowns, social events, the proud, loving faces of family and friends to witness and record on film an exciting program—marks the end of one of life's most important chapters. Moreover, it's a chapter that helps launch these AP graduates on career paths that can carry them to the highest pinnacles in their industry.

But the end of one chapter also leads, as it must with inexorable progress, to life's next chapter. Now is the time for all good graduates to come to their *own* aid; a reality check that exposes them to the outside world.

Fortunately, not only has Academy Pacific prepared them well for their excursion into the real world, but the school takes an active role in what happens to its graduates as they enter that outside world. Like all other facets of an Academy Pacific education—a lifetime commitment for updating their training as often as they wish and as long as they continue in the industry of their choice—placement is not only an immediate commitment, but can even afford lifetime support down often convoluted career paths.

"I know I'm going to place every one of them," says Paul Favreau, the school's Director of Placement. "When I brief each entering group of students I tell them 'there's a job for everybody in this room,'" Favreau says with the confidence of someone who has been the school's principal placement specialist for nearly five years. Before coming to Academy Pacific, Favreau spent twenty years with placement agencies. "I really enjoy placing people, matching them with positions that will bring the greatest satisfaction for both sides." Favreau says the average placement time for graduates is within three months of their graduation ceremonies.

Beaming AP graduates, all capped and gowned, 1993.

Naval Sea Cadet Color Guard, led graduation processional, Hollywood Roosevelt Hotel, 1995.

Diplomas readied for presentation, AP graduation, 1996.

AP graduate welcomes Burbank-Glendale Airport reps at Alumni dinner, Marina del Rey, 1995.

AP's placement record for recent years seems to back up Favreau's enthusiasm. In 1994, for example, the placement rate was 82 percent. Recognize that was during a period—the mid-1990s—many considered to be a worldwide economic downturn, some even used the dreaded term "recession." However, evidence in the latter 1990s is that people are traveling even more than ever. According to the nonprofit Travel Industry Association of America (TIAA), the number of individual trips of at least one hundred miles taken by Americans in the summer of 1996 was at least two percent ahead of the record-breaking summer of '95. For example, seat occupancy or "load factor" on airline flights for July of '96 was 74.3 percent, an increase of nearly three percent over the same period the year before. According to the Air Transport Association, the airline industry's trade group, load factor for all U.S. airlines was more than 71 percent in 1996, well ahead of any year since World War II.

The European Travel Commission predicted a record 4.9 million American visitors for the summer of '96, with more than 9 million for the entire year. That breaks all previous records. Individual airlines were reporting record bookings within the United States, to Europe as well as to Hawaii and the Far East. These record numbers were, of course, affecting the hospitality industry. Marriott and other leading hoteliers were reporting occupancy rates as high as 80 percent—with an industry average 9.2 percent higher for the summer of 1996 than the previous year.

Of particular interest to graduates, students and prospects for Academy Pacific—and to the industries it serves—is statistical evidence that Americans increasingly regard travel and tourism as a significant and important element of their lifestyle. Trips taken by Americans increased 45 percent from 1985 to 1995, according to

Founder/Director Marsha Toy at wheel of Excaliber, 1992.

TIAA, even as the population grew approximately 10 percent.

But the 1990s boom in travel and tourism is not only generated by Americans. Citizens of other nations are increasingly visiting the United States. In one of the world's biggest booming economies, South Korea, 613,000 citizens of that country visited the United States in 1995, spending more than $1 billion on hotel rooms, meals and souvenirs. The number of South Korean visitors to the U.S. has nearly tripled from 1991 to 1995. According to International Air Travel Association projections, more than 50 percent of the world's 736 million international airline passengers will be flying to, from or within the Asia-Pacific region. This projection does not even include mainland China. One Hong Kong-based

The "Sampson Sisters" at LAX ready to be wheeled aboard for flight to Hawaii, 1995.

consultant notes that six major airports, each with a capacity of 25 million annual passengers, are being built in Asia.

With the continuing growth of travel and tourism as a backdrop, personal enthusiasm of the potential for graduates and the involvement of all the AP staff, including the Director of Placement, is expressed by Favreau: "The most rewarding part of my job is when someone says to me, 'I got the job; I start next week.'"

TWA Clipped Wings President Marsha Toy with funds for Cystic Fibrosis Foundation, 1956.

RIGHT PAGE: ***Become involved in your community and your community will get involved with you**, noted Marsha Toy as school staff adopted cleaning and care of Apollo XI stars at Hollywood and Vine, 1987.*

There is a continuing, long term interest in AP students and graduates by Marsha Toy and the school's professional staff. Ample demonstration of the dedication is Favreau's comment, "I never give up until I place a graduate; it's an 'open book' to me." Most importantly, graduates have a lifetime commitment from AP for both continuing education/upgrading and placement. That is a basic tenet of the school that everyone on the staff understands and supports.

Loyalty is also a major factor for AP graduates. More than thirty-two years ago an AP graduate entered the travel business (Marsha Toy was his "placement director"). He recently hired a current AP graduate. In addition to his loyalty to the school, he also credits Marsha Toy with his success, noting, "I wouldn't be in my own business now if it weren't for that woman." Although his 32-year dedication may be a record, Favreau says he regularly works with graduates from the eighties and even seventies. "I treat people who came here ten, fifteen or even twenty years ago just like I do a brand new graduate."

Addressing the issue of the school's strict dress code, Favreau notes: "Prospective employers love to see evidence of that (dress code) when they come to interview. Most of them require uniform dress on duty so they visualize how their potential employees will look. Our dress code has always helped me in placement."

As expected, Favreau has a lengthy list–more than five hundred companies, he notes–of potential employers. Under the category he refers to as "Frequent Employers," Favreau rattles off agencies such as Brendan Tours, JetSet Tours, Uniworld Global Travel, Larchmont Travel, airlines such as Avia Tucker, Cocker, Tower, Mexicana, TACA, Malaysia, Cathay Pacific, Vanguard, Reno, in addition to well-known United and TWA. His placement "regulars" also include Crystal Cruises plus Radisson, Red Lion, InterContinental, Summit and Vagabond hotels, together with rental car agencies such as Budget, National and Avis. Of interest is the fact that many of these employers already have AP graduates on staff and are sufficiently impressed with AP people that they call Favreau saying, "I need six or seven people." One Central American airline, for example, has 95 percent AP graduates as passenger service agents, including even the LAX assistant station manager.

Airlines will always provide some level of their own, unique training for flight attendants to ensure that those serving in that carrier's cabin are familiar with their particular procedures. Major U.S. airlines—American, United, TWA, for example—have their own flight attendant schools. However, AP flight attendant graduates are welcomed by *all* airlines because the school teaches basics, cutting down significantly on training time with their eventual employer airline. AP flight attendant graduates "have a much better chance because of their training," says Favreau. With a number of smaller carriers or charter operators, "They're more than anxious to hire from us since we provide our flight attendant graduates with more training than they themselves can provide," Favreau observes. He estimates that, with AP flight attendant training, graduates have better than ninety percent chance of being hired.

Working an active group of sixty or seventy graduates at any given time, Favreau knows he can place AP-trained people—either for the first time or for those who want to change jobs or even careers.

A typical AP graduate has been carefully schooled in the details of their chosen travel, tourism or hospitality industry, has learned through hands-on tutoring several

LOS ANGELES AREA CHAMBER OF COMMERCE
404 SOUTH BIXEL STREET, P.O. BOX 3696 · LOS ANGELES, CALIFORNIA 90054 · (213) 482-4010

December 16, 1968

Miss Marsha Toy
2020 Castilian Drive
Hollywood, Calif. 90028

Dear Miss Toy:

The time has come to say a most sincere
thank-you to all the wonderful women on our Women's
Division Board of Directors for 1968. I hope you feel,
as I do, that we can be very proud of the professional
quality of our many accomplishments.

Our Board terms are for one year, as you
know. Invitations to serve on the Board for the following
year are extended by the new president and her officers.

The 1968 Executive Committee joins me in
expressing our deepest appreciation for your valuable
contribution this year, and in wishing you a joyous,
successful new year.

Cordially,

Laura Walters

Laura Walters
President/1968
WOMEN'S DIVISION

LWalters:gg

*Recognition from Los Angeles Area Chamber of
Commerce, 1968.*

June 30, 1993

Marsha Toy
President & Founder
Academy Pacific Business and Travel College
1777 North Vine St.
Hollywood, CA 90028

Dear Marsha:

On behalf of the Chamber, I would again like to congratulate you on
your accomplishments as a Hollywood "Woman in Business". We were
very impressed with your extensive resume.

We hope you enjoyed the luncheon with Gayle Wilson. We thought you
might like a photo to commemorate the event and are enclosing one
with this letter. Best wishes with your career.

Sincerely,

Michael Dubin
President

MD:ma

/enclosure

7000 Hollywood Boulevard ● Suite 1 ● Hollywood, California 90028 ● (213) 469-8311 ● FAX (213) 469-2805

*Congratulations from Hollywood Chamber for
"Women in Business" award to Marsha Toy, 1993.*

California Governor's wife, Gayle Wilson, presents "Women in Business" plaque to Marsha Toy, 1993.

*AP students volunteer and receive customer service training at PBS KCET-TV
Pledge Nights, 1995.*

Travelers Aid Society of Los Angeles Magellan Award is presented to TASLA 1st Vice President Marsha Toy, 1994.

RIGHT PAGE: **Marsha Toy "runs" in Los Angeles Marathon on Hollywood Boulevard; AP sponsored Marathon breakfast for Travelers Aid volunteers, 1992.**

industry computer systems, has had the opportunity to gain actual experience or working observation in the "field," understands and practices the highest grooming and dress standards imposed by the school, and practices the ethical standards established by the Director and carried out by the professional staff. In short, by all measures, AP graduates move into a burgeoning industry with heads held high, confident in the knowledge they are well prepared.

AP graduates are well prepared principally because of the faculty, the driving force in the school's classrooms. Ultimately, the teaching staff educates and inspires the student body, taking note of unique needs and talents, sharing observations and evaluations with fellow staff members to carry out the basic AP concept that "students come first!"

In addition to a wide range of advanced degrees in such subjects as psychology, sociology, international business, political science, economics, languages, including oral and written English, the teaching staff has a combined total of more than 250 years on-the-job experience including airlines, hotels, cruise lines, tour companies, travel agencies and government tourism authorities. AP teachers are participants at every school event. They are involved. For the entire Academy Pacific professional staff, preparing students for their professional careers is a way of life.

Each of the forty-five member Academy Pacific staff is imbued with their inspiration directly from the school's founder and director, Marsha Toy.

Mrs. Toy, as everyone at the school calls her (even out of earshot), is personally involved with the day-to-day operation of the school, providing overall direction. She writes policy, defines standards and works at all levels. She is a constant reminder that the objective of the staff is to do what is best for the students and for the school. However, once standards are established, she delegates responsibility for executing tasks. One staffer says: "She is as tenacious as any man I have ever worked with!"

Despite her disclaimer in the 1930s that "teaching" was not a career she wanted to pursue, education has become her life. "Teacher" is perhaps the most apt single word to describe Marsha Toy. "If you want to see her get excited, watch her teach," one staff member observed. She is generous with her knowledge and experience whether it's with individual students or the staff. "I believe the secret of life is not resenting people or things. I never become angry or resentful." That philosophy has resulted in significant success for Academy Pacific and its founder and director, Marsha Toy. A hallmark of Mrs. Toy's caring is her annual, "writ-by-hand" Christmas letter to friends and compatriots worldwide.

The basic policies and tenets of the school come down from the top. The personal tutoring and frequent financial assistance to individuals who are quietly struggling but ultimately graduate and go out into the business world are hallmarks of AP caring.

In addition to internal support for students, under Mrs. Toy's guidance the school and its professional staff reach out to the community, doing the right thing!

Academy Pacific actively supports a Southern California home for disadvantaged and orphaned youth, Hollygrove Children's Home. AP students and the school host an annual holiday festival, including a special dinner and presents for Hollygrove's youngsters.

Chinese students sponsored by Marsha Toy (right) with Los Angeles Airport Commissioner Sam Greenberg, former LAX General Manager Fran Fox, Los Angeles Mayor Tom Bradley, 1986.

Toy exults at the keyboard, 1992.

On field trip to Goodyear Blimp with AP Admissions Director Sandi Dover, 1992.

At Malibu beach with great niece Mariana and great nephew Tommy, 1996.

In addition, AP students and staff actively work at Travelers Aid's Teen Canteen in Hollywood. Mrs. Toy has served for many years (several times as vice president) on the Board of Directors of the Travelers Aid Society of Los Angeles. She served as president of the Los Angeles chapter of TWA Clipped Wings, an organization of former TWA flight attendants (known in Sammy's era as "air hostesses"). In addition, she has chalked up lengthy service on the Aero Club of Southern California's Board of Directors. She has encouraged—often subsidized—AP students to become members of the Aero Club. AP students are regularly in competition for the Aero Club's annual scholarships.

An act of compassion that was quietly achieved by Mrs Toy was bringing to the United States three young Chinese students, helping to finance their education in America, and then seeing that they found jobs. She has made possible U.S. citizenship and gainful employment for other young people who could be classified as true mixed ethnicity.

Many of these community support activities are quiet, behind-the-scenes efforts. Not so the school's (and specifically the ET) regular participation in Public Broadcasting's KCET Pledge Drives. AP students are in the KCET studio, manning phones, recording pledges and generally supporting the celebrity guests who serve as hosts and "guest pitchmen" for KCET Pledge Drives.

The concept that "Students Come First!" is evident throughout the school. As Mrs. Toy expresses it, "They are our customers and we let them know that. We tell them, 'We're here working for you...at your service....make use of that support.'"

For the Academy Pacific professional staff that basic tenet is evident in all of its efforts. It underscores the operation of the school. ✈

THE NEARLY FIFTY YEARS OF STEADY GROWTH AND PROGRESS OF ACADE-
my Pacific Travel College have culminated in a highly professional, established
teaching institution carefully preparing 340 annual graduates to move confidently
into the burgeoning travel, tourism and hospitality industries.

In its own building not far from the site where it all began in 1948, the school's
expansive classrooms, teaching laboratories and the computer-oriented facilities
available to its professional staff of teachers and administrators assure that AP is
more than prepared to meet the challenges of these growth industries during the
balance of the twentieth and well into the twenty-first century.

Equipped with data from a wide range of impartial industry trade organizations
and consultants, Marsha Toy recently observed: "It's staggering to the mind what
has happened to our industry!" Every facet of the business—airlines, cruise ships,
tours, hotels and the entire infrastructure such as travel agencies and car rental companies—is expanding. The bright picture for Academy Pacific graduates is the
career and employment opportunities presented by this "staggering" growth.

However, the rapidly growing industries, cognizant of the necessity for positive
images with the buying public, are carefully and judiciously choosing individuals for
their professional staffs. Owners and managers of the wide range of travel and
tourism service businesses competing for the general public's discretionary dollars
(or pesos or francs or marks) are acutely aware of the need to "put their best foot
forward" as they select personnel.

Those who hire give high marks to applicants whose first impression exudes
confidence and a professional appearance. Following that initial impression that a
well-groomed applicant makes, skilled interviewers quickly determine level of
knowledge of the particular industry. Interviewers are particularly impressed with
applicants who display a knowledge of the company and of the job under consideration. Although they may know that an applicant has done his or her "homework"
in preparation for the interview, they are nonetheless impressed with the fact the
applicant has gone the "extra mile." Skilled interviewers also recognize a positive
attitude, confidence and high self-esteem. Being ill-prepared for the growth markets
of the next ten to twenty years can doom a career.

The professional staff of faculty and administrators at Academy Pacific are uniquely dedicated to the education and training of students who can move with confidence into the *real* world of travel, tourism and hospitality.

The school's slogan that *Students Come First* is a way of life. Academy Pacific graduates are well-prepared to meet the high standards of the companies with whom they seek employment. ✈

❁ Index ❁

Wilkinsburg, Pennsylvania, 13, 16, 18, 35, 43, 48

Wilson, Chairman, 33

Wilson, Gayle, 110

Wilson, Meredith, 51

Wilson, T. B., 31, 33

Wisconsin, 47

Women in Business, 109

Womens Airforce Service Pilots (WASPS), 43

World War II, 104

Worldspan, 68

Wright, Theon, 33

Y

Yorty, Sam, 66

Z

Zanover, Martha, 36

IN ADDITION TO AIRPORTS AND AVIATION ARTICLES, MR. SCHONEBERGER has authored or co-authored six books (*Seven Decades of Progress; California Wings; Out of Thin Air; Allison Power of Excellence,* two volumes; *Call Me Pat*) ; served as editorial consultant on another (*Herman the German*); and is currently working on a biography of an aviation pioneer.

He spent seventeen years with GE Aircraft Engines; and eight as Northrop corporate director of communications.

Mr. Schoneberger is past president and director, Aero Club of Southern California (NAA, FAI); past president of Aero Exhibits Inc., owner of Hughes Flying Boat; member, Collier Trophy selection committee; director, Flight Path Learning Center of Southern California; Aviation/Space Writers Association (AWA), Society of Aerospace Communicators (SAC) director; was AWA international director, Awards Committee chairman. He graduated from the University of South Carolina; and attended Miami University (Ohio) and the University of Cincinnati. ✈